FELA & Rai

What Every P

By Reshard J. Alexander, Esq., MBA, LL.M

RJ Alexander Law, PLLC

7676 Hillmont Street #240Q

Houston, Texas 77040

Phone: (832) 458-1756

Email: rja@rjalexanderlaw.com

Website:http://rjalexanderlaw.com

FELA & Railroad Injury Law:

Table of Contents

-
-
-
-
-
-
-
-
-
-
-
-

Disclaimer:

This book provides general information to the public about Federal Employees Liability Act lawsuits and personal injury-related railroad claims. This book is not intended to serve as advice, take the place of you seeking a consultation from a lawyer in person, or create an attorney-client relationship. To create and attorney-client relationship, you should seek an initial consultation and then sign a written attorney-client agreement that documents and establishes the terms of the agreement. The book is distributed, given, and/or sold with the notion that the author/publisher is not in any capacity rendering legal advice or professional services to the reader. In the event that you are suffering from a legal issue, you should consult with and retain the services of a competent personal injury lawyer.

There are no warranties given regarding the completeness or accuracy of this book as it relates to your particular legal concern. The book was not designed to replace the advice of a licensed lawyer or suited for any one purpose in the legal arena. The sale or promotion of this book does not create any additional warranties, obligations, or agreement with the author, published, or legal entity owned or employing the aforementioned. This book is not intended to cover every legal issue that might arise in your life. The author/publisher shall not be liable in any form or fashion for damages for your actions after reading this book.

Dedication:

I dedicate this book to my family. "Hovi is home, all these phonies are coming to a halt."- Jay-Z, 4.44

Foreword:

We are living in a world that is losing its' mind. Corporate greed is entrenched within our American social, economic, and political system. We praise business gurus for their ability to churn out large amounts of money when wage inequality is worse than ever. Automobile safety measures are cut in favor of stockholders' profit and we as a nation have accepted these items as the norm. Tort reform has scaled back the ability of plaintiffs to seek fair redress for medical malpractice cases and auto insurance companies are forcing people to consider arbitration clauses in new policies.

I wrote this book to give railroad workers and vehicle injury victims a resource to review when faced with a railroad injury. I have been a licensed Texas lawyer for six years and assisted clients in a variety of areas.

Personal injury law is by far one of the most difficult and yet satisfying areas to practice. Nationally, it seems that many lawyers list personal injury law as one of the areas that they practice, but do not actually handle many cases in this area. Railroad injury law is an even more nuanced area that requires added focus on this particular area of law. Oftentimes, lawyers state that they practice family, criminal, and personal injury law or some sort of combination to keep the lights on at the office. While this is understandable from a business financial standpoint, as a client this can put you at a severe disadvantage when choosing a lawyer who does not primarily practice personal injury and FELA railroad law.

It is disheartening when people come to my law office and they have went to a lawyer who does not focus on railroad injury and personal injury cases. Potential clients have been led to believe they do or do not have a case and then when they seek assistance from my firm I must turn them away because the case has been botched in some manner or the statute of limitations has passed thus barring them by law from any form of compensation.

Meet My Firm:

Before attending law and business graduate school, I obtained my undergraduate degree with a double major in Political Science and English with a minor Economics from the University of North Carolina at Charlotte. I graduated from West Virginia University School of Law and College of Business with a JD and MBA in 2010. Afterwards, I graduated from the University of Houston Law Center in 2012 with a Masters of Law in Energy, Environmental, and Natural Resources Law. I started my own law firm as soon as I was licensed as a lawyer in 2011. I am not originally from Houston, Texas.

My hometown is Charlotte, North Carolina, but I was first exposed to the great state of Texas through Longhorn football. After I graduated from high school, I enlisted into the Armed Forces via the North Carolina Army National Guard. My basic training began with my fellow enlistees and me being run out of cattle cars in the middle of the night into Army barracks in Lawton, Oklahoma. I would stay there for approximately six months graduating at the top of my basic training enlistment group and with the highest scores for my Advanced Initial Training (AIT) Military Occupational Specialty (MOS).

During my time in Lawton, Oklahoma, the drill sergeants allowed us to attend the Red River Shootout between the Oklahoma Sooners and Texas Longhorns. I knew that I was destined to live in the state of Texas so after graduating from law school during the one of the worst economic recessions that our country has ever faced I seized the moment to make the jump to the Lone Star state. I have practiced law in the state of Texas for almost five years and plan on doing so for many more years to come.

When you visit my law firm site, you will will immediately notice that I focus on personal injury law. During the first few years of my practice I handled a variety of cases so I have had some time to decide what I would like to focus on. I have taken the last two years to work with more seasoned personal injury lawyers in some capacity to fill any gaps in my knowledge. Employing an outsider's perspective to Texas law and the actual practice of personal injury law, I have created a system that ushers your FELA Act / railroad injury case through the proper channels and ensures that your lawsuit is timely managed.

Texas Tort Reform and Medical Malpractice:

Texans are an interesting group of people. Politics in the state: even more eclectic. The politics of the state are conservative and this stems from the rugged frontier that once composed the Texas landscape and the pioneering, self-sufficient streak that has existed here since the state was a once an independent country. The type of people that would move to this section of the world, not knowing what awaited them, were a hardy people who as risk-takers learned to depend on themselves rather than state or federal assistance. "A 'health care liability claim' means a cause of action against a health care provider or physician for treatment, lack of treatment, or other claimed departure from accepted standards of medical care, or health care, or safety or professional or administrative services directly related to health care, which proximately results in injury to or death of a claimant, whether the claimant's claim or cause of action sounds in tort or contract." Texas Civil Practice & Remedies Code: Medical Liability: Definitions: Title 4, Chapter 74, Section 74.013.

Wow. What does that even mean, right?! Well, this is the definition of a medical malpractice claim in Texas. Years ago, our leading politicians in Texas deprived many (past, present, and possibly future) people who are injured by medical professionals from receiving proper compensation for injures because the care of the attending/operating medical professional was not up to par to that of the average medical professional in the community. Caps were placed on the amount of money that someone could receive as a result of a medical malpractice claim. This means that if you lose sight in both eyes and I lose the use of my hand, both as the result of medical negligence that the most either of us could receive from a negligent party is $250,000.00.

Yet, all it is not lost. Some lawyers still practice medical malpractice law and will fight for you to collect proper compensation in these types of situations. If you ever suffer an injury such as this feel free to call me at **(832) 458-1756** or email the firm at <u>rja@rjalexanderlaw.com</u>

Car, Motorcycle, and Truck Accident Cases:

Auto accident law is the foundation that many personal injury lawyers build their practices around. I have placed a large part of my practice into properly handling car wreck cases. These situations are time-consuming for auto railroad injury victims and place huge mental, physical, and financial burdens on him/her while recovering from injury. I have written a book that is specifically tailored for Texas auto railroad injury victims. If you or a loved has been injured in a motor vehicle purchase my book, Texas Car, Motorcycle, and Truck Accident Law: What Every Victim Must Know (available now on Amazon Kindle and paperback).

Distracted Driving Cases:

Distracted Driving is becoming a silent national catastrophe for young drivers and those who are social-media involved. Distracted driving is defined as any activity that could divert a person's attention away from the primary task of driving. Distracted driving is not limited to attempting to capture the latest Pokemon on the roadways, but includes:

- Cellphone Usage

- Eating and Drinking

- Watching Videos

- Reprimanding Children

- Using GPS

- Smoking

The rise of smart-phones have spiked a rise in the injury of people on our Texas highways, toll ways and public roads. According to the Texas Department of Transportation, over 100,000 traffic collisions happen every year due to distracted driving. In 2015, over 10% of Texas motor railroad injuries were due to distracted driving. AAA now states that 25-50% of vehicle railroad injuries due to distracted driving.

So, if you are involved in a vehicle collision it is likely that the other driver was engaging in some secondary activity outside of driving his/her vehicle. It is imperative that you drive defensively when you are operating your vehicle. You cannot predict the behavior of others on the road and so you must always think of the dumbest thing that neighboring drivers could do and plan accordingly.

Drunk Driving Cases:

There is no other legally ingested substance that has produced more motor vehicle deaths in the United States than alcohol. According to CDC (Center for Disease Control) in 2013 alone, over 10,000 people were killed in alcohol-impaired collisions across the United States of America. Over one-third (over 10,000) of the people killed that year died as a result an alcohol-related railroad injury. Nationally, everyday 28 people perish in alcohol-involved crashes. One person every 53 minutes. The costs related to dealing with drunk driving amount to at least 44 billion.

We are dealing with a national crisis that could be avoided by not drinking and driving, limiting your alcohol intake at social functions, designating a sober driver before attending an event, or calling a taxi to take you home. Drunk driving deaths are not "accidents" in the traditional sense of the word. These situations do not arise because they are unavoidable. These happen because someone makes a conscious decision to drive intoxicated.

More Texas DUI-related crashes are reported between the hours of 2am and 3am on Saturday morning than any other time of the week according to 2015 crash statistics gathered by the Texas Department of Transportation. When you are injured in a car railroad injury that is due to the negligence of another person and he/she is drunk at the time of the occurrence, you may be awarded punitive damages for your suffering. Call RJ Alexander Law, PLLC to discuss the case at **(832) 458-1756**. If you are injured then I can come to you and visit you at your home if necessary.

Drunk driving is considered a serious criminal offense in the state of Texas. The first two offenses are treated as misdemeanors. Afterwards, each driving while intoxicated offense is a felony. All offenses are punishable by fines and jail time. Additionally, those persons injured by drunk drivers are entitled to civil compensatory damages in a court of law. This is an attempt to give the victimized party compensation for the injuries he/she sustained at the hands of the wrongdoer. , Texas law also allows victims of drunk driving to receive compensation through punitive damages. Punitive damages seek to punish the negligent party for gross negligence and deter parties from such behavior in the future. While these damages rarely make the injured party completely whole, they assist in the recovery of injury in cases that usually involve serious personal damage.

As a personal injury lawyer, a great deal of my legal practice is focused on motor vehicle accident law. If you are facing serious injuries as a result of a drunk driver hitting your vehicle feel free to give my law firm, RJ Alexander Law, PLLC, a call at **(832) 458-1756** or email me [rja@rjalexanderlaw.com] to set up an appointment.

Dog Bite Cases:

Texas is one of the leading dog bite injury cases in the United States. Rottweilers and Pit Bulls lead the number of fatal dog attacks in the United States, but dog bites/attacks occur with a variety of breeds. My law firm handles dog bites and attack personal injury cases. I have written a book that is available now on Amazon Kindle and paperback format that helps you in the event that you or a loved one is the victim of a dog bite: Texas Dog Bite Law: What Every Victim Must Know (available on Amazon Kindle and paperback).

Bicycle Accident Cases:

Since focusing on personal injury cases, RJ Alexander Law, PLLC has taken an active role in bicycle accident litigation. Houston, Texas has seen a tragic number of people who have die or become injured by bicycle riding through the city. All lives are valuable whether in a motor vehicle, bicycling, or walking as a pedestrian and because of this I have volunteered with Houston Ghost Bike. Ghost Bike is an organization that strives to promote awareness among the general populace about the number of bicyclists who are killed each year as a result of fatal motor vehicle operation.

The effects of getting hit on a bicycle versus inside the confines of an automobile are obvious. Someone riding a bicycle does not have a steel and/or fiberglass body protecting them from direct collision. A bicyclist does not have the benefit of front or side airbags to cushion the blow of striking the hard concrete with his/her body. There is no on-board system to alert emergency services of a possible life threatening situation. Many drivers have often hit bicyclists in the Houston area and left the person clinging to life in a ditch on the side of the road. Sometimes the bicycle is the injured person's only means of transportation, but it does not matter happen how it happens--hitting someone on a bicycle is a serious concern and so it must be treated as such by all drivers.

If you are involved in a Texas bicycle accident, call my firm at RJ Alexander Law, PLLC or pick up my book, <u>Texas Car, Motorcycle, and Truck Accident Law: What The Injured Must Know</u> (available now on Amazon Kindle and paperback format). Bicycle accidents often involved the least fortunate of us, children, and young adults. When you see a bicycle on the road or you are in an area that bicyclists are known to frequent please slow down on the road and give the rider the same respect that you would give a car. Better yet, pretend that it was your child, father, or grandmother on that bicycle.

FELA & Maritime Offshore Injury Cases:

One of my latest books, <u>FELA and Maritime Offshore Injury: What Every Worker Must Know</u> (available on Amazon Kindle and paperback), helps seamen who are injured in maritime settings with a resource that they can use to maximize their FELA or maritime injury claim and quickly realize when it might be better to have a personal injury lawyer that focuses on handling FELA cases and maritime law claims.

Please understand that this book does not cover the Longshore and Harbor Workers' Compensation Act. If you are a longshoreman and injured by while working then you need to seek the help of someone who specializes in this particular statute.

Nevertheless, there are a few differences between the FELA and Longshore and Harbor Worker's Compensation Act that I may be able to clarify for you in this introduction. The FELA basically applies when a seamen has been injured in connection to his/her line of employment on a railroad. When the worker is a land-based employee and not connected to a railroad or fleet of railroads then he/she is likely covered under the LHWCA regarding available compensation.

The Longshore and Harbor Workers Compensation Act (LHWCA) is a federal statute enacted by in 1927 to protect land-based maritime workers. These workers are generally not covered by the FELA. The LHWCA allows land-based maritime workers to receive temporary compensation totaling 2/3 of their average weekly salary while completing medical treatment. The injured worker may then receive 2/3 of his/her lost wage earning capacity or compensation for sustained injuries.

Feel free to call me at **(832) 458-1756** for a free consultation regarding your injury to determine whether you qualify as a seamen or longshoreman.

Product Liability, Class Action, & Mass Tort Cases:

If you or a loved one are injured by a defective product my upcoming book will provide you with the knowledge to help you recover compensation and hold the product manufacturer accountable for your injuries. Product Liability, Class Action, & Mass Tort Law: What Every Consumer Must Know (available December 2017).

Refinery Accidents and Industrial Disaster Cases:

I am a huge lover of the outdoors. In a world of computers, smart-phones, and all-knowing technology that as a society we are losing our ability to connect to nature. When I attended law school in West Virginia, I would often take long hikes with my family on the weekends in the surrounding forests around Morgantown, WV. My dream was to represent defenseless people who are injured by industrial disasters by huge corporations. I interned with non-profits where I assisted farmers who had toxic sludge dumped onto their farming areas by waste management companies.

Some memories stay with you a lifetime and leave deep impressions on what type of lawyer you want to be and who you want to represent. After graduating from West Virginia University, I matriculated into the University of Houston Law Center to further my knowledge in Energy and Environmental Law and represent those who are injured by corporate malfeasance. My book, <u>Refinery Accidents and Industrial Disaster Law: What Every Employee Must Know</u> (available November 2017). This book was written to help those who need help with handling refinery and chemical plant, gas pipeline explosions, and wrongful death matters.

Community Involvement:

I pride myself on the fact that since graduating from law school I have been very active in giving back to the community in the form of pro bono services. While enrolled at the University of Houston Law Center, I frequently helped with the

Veteran's Clinic at the local Veteran Affairs hospital providing pro bono consultations to fellow veterans and their family members. After graduating from UH Law Center, I assisted at the Shape Center Legal Clinic for over three years each Saturday giving pro bono consultations on issues ranging from real estate to criminal law matters. Recently, starting in January 2016, I created the Acres Homes Legal Clinic. The clinic provides pro bono consultations for all types of law one night a week. I plan to establish book scholarships at West Virginia University College of Law and the University of Houston Law Center by 2018 to assist future lawyers who come from working class backgrounds.

I have served on City of Houston Land Assembly Redevelopment Authority Board, various Chamber of Commerce boards, and non-profit associations. I established the Minority Trial Lawyers Association, a networking function for lawyers to meet, refer cases, and share knowledge.

In regards to personal injury law service, I am a member of the Texas Trial Lawyers Association. This is a legal organization that is dedicated to representing consumers and victims of corporate and individual harm caused by others. TTLA has always fought to ensure that the rights guaranteed by our Constitution are protected, namely the seventh amendment that guarantees the right to a trial by jury, and to ensure that ordinary citizens are represented in the legislative process. I am a member of the Houston Trial Lawyers Association. HTLA serves as the local extension of TTLA and promotes the same principles of justice, equality, and cooperation among lawyers are preserved for the public-at-large.

Introduction:

This book was written to provide workers and civilians who are injured in railroad setting with a resource that they can use to maximize their FELA claim or railroad injury claim. Additionally, they may quickly realize by reading this book when it might be better to have a personal injury lawyer that focuses on handling FELA claims and railroad injury lawsuits.

The Federal Employers' Liability Act is a federal law passed in 1908 to help railroad workers who are injured while working for railroad companies. FELA provides redress for railroad employees by providing them the ability to bring a lawsuit in federal or state court. Although this law is reviled by railroad companies because it allows injured workers to seek proper compensation, it is likely to remain around a long time as it has the backing of the Republican-led Congress.

The book not only provides a guide for injured railroad workers, but informs civilians (those not employed by a railroad company) about how to best handle a railroad-grade crossing wreck. If you are involved in an automobile, bicycle, or pedestrian wreck, you should continue to the chapters designated for your particular situation.

This book does **NOT** go into detail regarding disability claims under the American Disabilities Act of 1990. A brief background for those of you facing disability claims under the ADA, American with Disabilities Act 1990 provides "a clear and comprehensive national mandate for elimination of discrimination against individuals with disabilities...." This protection in employment and the transportation sector is extended to railroad company employees.

Railroad workers are protected from employment discrimination under the ADA. In order to prove discrimination under the ADA:

1. you must have a qualifying disability,

2. Be able to perform the essential functions of the position in question with or without reasonable accommodation, and

3. Have an action taken against you by the employer due to the disability.

This is a fundamental test for proving employment discrimination. However, this is not all you may be required to show in order to win your case. Consult with an employment lawyer or your designated legal counsel for further instruction.

Additionally, this book does **NOT** cover trespassers and railroad wrongful-death cases. I will likely update this book to cover this topic in the second edition.

Feel free to call me at **(832) 458-1756** for a free consultation regarding your injury to determine whether you qualify as a civilian or railroad worker.

RESOURCES

Association of American Railroads

Federal Railroad Administration

National Labor Relations Board

National Transportation Safety Board

Operation Lifesaver

Railroad Retirement Board

US Department of Transportation

US Department of Labor

RAILROAD EMERGENCY NUMBERS

Always call 911 and/or the local enforcement agency first!

Amtrak	**1-800-331-0008**
BNSF Railway	**1-800-832-5452**
CSX Transportation	**1-800-232-0144**
Canadian National	**1-800-465-9239**
Canadian Pacific	**1-800-716-9132**
Kansas City Southern	**1-800-892-6295**
Norfolk Southern	**1-800-453-2530**
Union Pacific Railroad	**1-888-877-7267**

Chapter 1: The History of Railroad Law and American Expansion

American Railroad History

No other mode of modern transportation has helped shape our young nation more than the locomotive and railroad system. Indeed, no other vehicle has been more responsible for the expansion of our country's borders. It has allowed us to transport food, natural resources, and manpower to once impossible to reach to places with a speed that was unparalleled at the time of its' inception. The railroad preserved our nation in the Civil War thanks to the highly developed rail infrastructure in the Northern part of the United States. On May 10, 1869, the completion of the Transcontinental Railroad at Promontory, Utah allowed our country to further blossom as the nation's population now had a safe route to expand further west. Today, the modern American railroad system encompasses more than 140,000 miles and allows iron chariots to traverse from sea to shining sea.

Originally, railroads competed with the American canal system as goods were initially brought to the states through a system of coastal importing/exporting, river ferrying, and man-made waterways. Over time, railroads would assume the peak position as America's transport system of choice. Initially, railroads started out as nothing more than horse-drawn carriages pulled along sets of wooden tracks (tramways) hauling coal or some other substance to and fro, but later morphed into steam-powered locomotives as technology pushed for faster, tireless, and sturdier vehicles. Although, the first railways began in Great Britain, the technology would eventually hit American shores when engineers and like-minded business individuals saw the potential for increased revenue and efficiency. You will notice that I didn't mention safety.

The history of the American railroad system could be traced to one particular railroad vehicle, The Best Friend of Charleston, the first domestically built locomotive to haul a passenger train. This piece of machinery would go on to create one of the first American casualties of the modern day railroad transport system when the boiler exploded because a local fireman decided to sit on the safety valve because he was tired of hearing the noise that it made.

Common Train Components and Personnel/Train Crew Responsibilities

These are the definitions of common train components according to the Federal Railroad Administration.

On-Track Rail Equipment:

Equipment Consist. An equipment consist is a train, locomotive(s), cut of cars, or a single car not coupled to another car or locomotive.

Car. A car is:

(1) Any unit of on-track equipment designed to be hauled by locomotives, or

(2) Any unit of on-track work equipment such as a track motorcar, highway-rail vehicle, push car, crane, or ballast tamping machine.

Locomotive. A locomotive is a piece of on-track equipment other than hi-rail, specialized maintenance, or other similar equipment:

(1) With one or more propelling motors designed for moving other equipment;

(2) With one or more propelling motors designed to carry freight or passenger traffic or both; or

(3) Without propelling motors but with one or more control stands.

Control Cab Locomotive. A locomotive without propelling motors but with one or more control stands. Note: A control [cab] car locomotive is to be counted as a car and not as a locomotive unit in the Rail Equipment Accident/Incident Report.

DMU Locomotive. A diesel-powered multiple-unit operated locomotive with one or more propelling motors designed to carry passenger traffic. Note: A DMU locomotive is to be counted as a car and not as a locomotive unit in the Rail Equipment Accident/Incident Report.

EMU Locomotive. An electric multiple-unit operated locomotive:

(1) With one or more propelling motors designed to carry freight or passenger traffic or both; or

(2) Without propelling motors but with one or more control stands.

Note: An EMU locomotive is to be counted as a car and not as a locomotive unit in the FRA Rail Equipment Accident/Incident Report.

Motorcar. A self-propelled unit of equipment designed to carry freight or passenger traffic. (Does not include track motor cars or similar work equipment.)

Train. For purposes of accident/incident reporting, a train is a locomotive or locomotives coupled with or without cars, and with or without markers displayed. This definition includes trains consisting entirely of self-propelled units designed to carry passengers, freight traffic, or both.

Yard Switching Trains. Trains operated primarily within yards for the purpose of switching other equipment. Examples include the making up or breaking up of trains, service industrial tracks within yard limits, storing or classifying cars, and other similar operations.

Work train. Work trains are non-revenue trains used for the administration and upkeep service of the railroad. Examples are: official trains, inspection trains, special trains running with a company fire apparatus to save the railroad's property from destruction, trains that transport the railroad's employees to and from work when no transportation charge is made, construction and upkeep trains run in connection with maintenance and improvement work, and material and supply trains run in connection with operations.

Terminal & Railyard Staff

A railroad terminal is a combination of different faculties that receive and send out trains when needed. The rail yard houses the differing track systems that switch freight/storage cars and put together different rail-cars. Many railroad injuries occur in these areas. Rail-yards have specific safety restrictions regarding the speed of cars and signaling the movement of cars.The best way to determine whether safety violations occurred is by examining the railroad company's Internal Control Plan (ICP).

There are a number of people who work in railroad terminals and rail-yards. I have included their titles and descriptions for a brief overview below:

Superintendent: responsible for the whole operation and may have managerial staff reporting to him/her.

Train Crew: the people responsible for maintaining the successful operation and maintenance of the train.

Chief Train Dispatcher: similar to an air traffic controller. He/she is responsible for the departure and arrivals of all train cars.

Train Dispatcher: reports to the Chief. Instructs trains on when they need to leave and arrive in particular destinations.

Road Foreman: The leader on the ground in the locomotive operations. Responsible for monitoring the movement of locomotives and instructing the crew.

Terminal Train-master: Ensures that the daily safety operations of the terminal or facility are obeyed.

Yardmaster: responsible for managing the rail-yard and the positioning of cars and tracks inside of the yard.

FELA and Railroad Law Fact:

The Best Friend of Charleston, tested in October of 1830, pulled train cars, the first locomotive to do so in the United States, along six miles of track out of Charleston.

Rail-yard & Terminal Facilities

Most rail-yards are major railroad companies consist of large tracts divided into multiple, smaller yards. In these yards, there are a number of operations that take place and many rail-yard employees are injured in these settings. I have listed some below:

Car shop: This is where train-cars are repaired.

Classification bowl: When the train cars make it over the hump in the rail-yard, the cars are separated along various tracks through a series of switches. They usually consists of more than 40 tracks with division of six to eight car classifications in each loop.

Hump yard: This is a rail-track that is on a "hump" in the rail-yard. The idea is that the hump engine attaches to the cars and distributes them over the hump along a main or lead track. The roll of gravity and accumulated speed when the cars are uncoupled from the hump engine allows them to move downhill at a rapid pace. This allows the train-cars to roll downhill into the classification bowl and proper class track after the air brakes are bled.

Fuel rack: This is where trains are fueled.

Flat Yard: Cars are pushed by a locomotive to their destination in the rail-yard in a rail-yard that is built on a flat surface.

Forwarding yard: The maintenance test and inspections are conducted here before a train departs and the train's end device are attached.

Receiving yard: This is where trains initially arrive. This yard removes the locomotive from the rest of the train and attaches a hump engine to the back of the cars.

Inter-modal terminal: This is where loads for the trains are added or taken out. These can be very dangerous areas for employees because lift equipment is used to handle the trailers.

Sand rack: This is where cars are filled with sand.

Constitutional Law and Railroads

Under the United States of America's Constitution, the legislative branch of our federal government (Congress) has the responsibility to regulate commerce between each and every state in our union. This can be found in Article I, Section 8, clause 3 and is generally referred to as the "Commerce Clause" in the legal community. Why does the federal government (U.S. Congress) have the ability to dictate the terms of how commerce is regulated in the entire United States? Because it allows us to create a nationwide system that passes resources throughout the nation in a responsible and uniform manner. Just think how crazy it would be if a train carrying hazardous materials needed to pass through six states and had to deal with six completely different environmental law settings. It would be chaos and likely ruin everything that makes America great!

Additionally, unlike many other forms of transportation, railroad regulation has always been deeply intertwined with regulation by the federal government. Railroad companies are losing market share in the resource and commercial transport industry to the heavy freight trucking industry. There are fewer regulations regarding rail operations than in past years. The federal government continues to exercise power over the railroad industry. State laws that attempt to regulate railroads are generally presumed valid, but these regulations are always secondary to any federal law on the area in question.

When state law comes steps onto the same track or issue as federal law and it covers anything regarding the railroad regulation from one state or another, state law is always takes a step back and must align with federal laws. The movement of goods across one state line to another is called interstate commerce. The federal agency that regulated railroads is called the Surface Transportation Board. Many cases have decided that when examining the power of states to regulate anything related to railroads or anything that may interfere with the interstate commerce of railroads that the Surface Transportation Board has final say and not state laws or agencies. These things can range from the ability of the state to enforce its' own environmental, tax, and/or state personal injury laws.

Preemption of State Laws Relating to Railroads - 130

We have already established that the railroad industry is governed by individual state law and national, federal laws. One example of this regulation is the Easterwood decision.

Basically, this United States Supreme Court case established that the Federal Railroad Safety Act preempts (takes precedence) over any reason that someone might bring a cause of action (lawsuit) in state court when it comes to railroad safety and the maximum allowable speed of train companies operating in interstate commerce.

In order to determine what is the federal government's authority regarding interstate commerce, the Supreme Court established a pre-emption test. Essentially, there are three variants of pre-emption (where the federal laws have final say over state law):

1. Field Preemption - This is where the federal law thoroughly occupies the law on the subject there is no room for the states to add anything to it.

2. Conflict Preemption - This is when federal and state law conflict on the issue at hand and the state is violating the U.S. Constitution's Supremacy Clause. This clause actually gives federal law higher favor in the eyes of the courts.

3. Express preemption - This is when a federal statute such as FELA explicitly states or implies that federal law will preempt state law.

In summation, federal law overshadows state law when it comes to regulating most railroad related matters.

FELA & Railroad Injury Law Tip:

Brakemen, shunters, and **switchers** have some of the most dangerous jobs in the railroad industry. If you are injured while employed in this line of work you should definitely contact your designated legal counsel (DLC) or union representative for assistance.

Chapter 2: What Is The Federal Employees Liability Act?

Federal Employers' Liability Act

Well, we are two chapters into the book and we are already getting to the heart of the matter. Railroad work is and has always been considered dangerous. At one point time in American history a railroad worker had a 1 in 35 chance of being injured on the job. The average life expectancy of a switch-man was only seven years on the job and a brakeman had less than a one in five chance of dying of natural causes. In 2016, there were over 780 casualties and 8,400 non-fatal railroad injuries.

In 1908, the Federal Employers' Liability Act commonly known as FELA was created. The first one was ruled unconstitutional in 1907 and updated in 1938. This law was created to minimize the increasing railroad worker injury and casualty rate and to shift some of the responsibility of these injuries to the railroad companies who did very little in the way of railroad safety. Indeed, as late as 2007, railroad workers who deal with switching, braking, and signal operations have a more than double fatality rate as the average

American worker. The Act was created because much like every other industry that involves manufacturing, heavy machinery, or procurement of natural resources, the corporations who employ these workers rarely thought of the safety of their workers.

How To Know If You Qualify As An Employee Under FELA

A railroader is entitled to recover damages from his company under the U.S. **Federal Employees' Liability Act if the following facts exist:**

1. The railroad he works for is engaged, even in small part, in interstate commerce; it either runs across states lines or handles interstate freight.

2. When injury to the worker is the result, even in part, of the negligence or carelessness of any officer, agent or employee of the railroad, or the injury is caused by any defect in the cars, engines, appliances, machinery, track, road bed, or any other equipment or the road.

Purpose of FELA

The Federal Employers' Liability Act, commonly referred to as "FELA," and found 45 U.S.C. § 51 gives railroad employees the right to seek monetary damages for injuries suffered in interstate commerce where the injury/injuries result in "whole or in part from the negligence of any of the officers, agents, or employees of [the railroad], or by reason of any defect, or insufficiency, due to its negligence, in its cars, engines, appliances, machinery, track, roadbed, works, boats, wharves or other equipment."

Liability

FELA is not considered a workers compensation law. When an railroad employee is injured, you are not entitled to immediate, automatic redress. However, under FELA you may bring a claim if your injury was caused by any way by the negligent acts by the railroad or its' employees. You must prove the injury was caused in some way by the railroad company which can be shown by demonstrating that the company failed to provide a safe work environment.

Under FELA case law, the railroad employer is responsible for:

1. providing a reasonably safe place to work

2. warning employees about unsafe work conditions

3. assigning workers to positions that they are actually able and qualified to perform

4. create and enforce safety rules.

Negligence

As stated above, the most common way to prove that the railroad company was at fault is by putting forth evidence that shows the employee was placed in an unreasonably dangerous place to work.

Railroad company negligence is:

1. shown by a lack of due care,

2. did what a person under the same, existing circumstance would not have done, or

3. failed to do what a reasonable and prudent person would ordinarily have done under similar circumstances.

The defendant/railroad company cannot transfer this safety standard to the plaintiff/railroad employee.

This negligence standard is not the same if there is a Federal Safety Appliance or Boiler Inspection Act violation as these both deal with the railroad failure to provide certain safety tools and equipment.

Employers' Duties

The railroad company MUST provide you with a safe working environment and tools that are in good working condition. You must show more than that you were hurt while at work. What is considered a safe working environment will ultimately be determined by a jury. One way to prove negligence by your employer is by demonstrating to the jury that there was a safer alternative to the way your work environment was conducted. No situation is the same. Therefore, always contact your union representative and/or a a personal injury lawyer that focuses on FELA claims.

Statute of Limitations

The statute of limitations is the time that you have to file a lawsuit seeking legal redress before your claim is forever barred from being heard in a court of law. The statute of limitations for a FELA claim is **exactly three years** from the day the injury occurred. If you are not aware of the injury or occupational disease that you are suffering, the statute of limitations will be suspended until the day that the injury is discovered. There must be "operative facts" that show you had knowledge of the occupational disease. Sometimes, things such as asbestos exposure may not show up until many years later. If you think that you are suffering an illness/occupational disease as a result of working for a railroad company then you should have your own medical doctor (not the company's doctor) give you a medical examination and have him/her recommend a specialist deals with the specific type of illness you are facing. DO NOT wait until you are a few months away from the statute of limitations demand to seek legal counsel regarding your potential lawsuit. Doing this will irreparably damage your chances of seeking maximum financial compensation for your injury/illness.

General Train Safety

Railroad safety regulations can be found in 49 Code of Federal Regulations 214 along with the civil fine violation costs. These regulations can cover issues ranging track safety such as inspection records, right of way issues, protective equipment, and track gauges/surfaces. Additionally, railroads will generally have their own individual safety regulations. It is best to secure a copy of this manual before your injury for your own records or if you are already injured as soon as possible.

Composition of FELA

Generally speaking, FELA is meant to be interpreted in a manner that grants the railroad worker some form of compensation if he/she can prove his/her case, especially considering that this is his/her only form of legal recourse when injured. Federal and state courts can both hear FELA lawsuits. When the claim is brought in federal court, the lawsuit can be heard in any district where the defendant resides, where the action arose, or where the defendant was doing business at the time the lawsuit is filed. In state court, a lawsuit can be filed in any state where the railroad company carries out business/solicits for business. Since it is a federal law, no matter where the claim is brought (federal or state court), federal law will control any substantive issues regarding the lawsuit. Additionally, local state rules cannot interfere with the procedural aspects of FELA.

Comparative Fault

FELA operates under a comparative fault statute, 45 U.S.C. § 53, which means even if the railroad employee contributes to his/her negligent injury, the employee may not be barred completely from seeking restitution. A jury can reduce your damages award in proportion to the negligence of the employee's actions in bringing about new conditions outside of the already existing ones that the railroad company created that caused his/her injury. The railroad company has the burden of proving that you contributed to your injury and it can't just say it. The company has to present evidence to back this allegation. Additionally, FELA has a "featherweight" standard of evidence meaning you just need to prove that the railroad employee was negligent in any way, no matter how slight, to prevail in your FELA claim. You are entitled to financial compensation for your injuries even if the employer only had a slight hand in causing your injury. The negligence of your co-worker causing your injury is attributed to your employer so you still have a FELA claim in these type of situations.

You will have a much easier time proving that the railroad employer was negligent by following my accident tips in the following chapters.

Assumption of risk

There is no assumption of the risk defense under 45 U.S.C. § 54. This means that the employer cannot argue that you "knew what were you getting into" or "that you knew the job was dangerous when you signed up."

Federal Safety Appliance Act

As railroads continued to grow after the Civil War, the rate of fatalities and catastrophic accidents among railroad personnel among railroad personnel exponentially grew. Many of the more serious incidents involved the coupling and uncoupling of railroad cars and the operation of manual handbrakes. Although states varied in the creation of legislation to handle this issue, Congress eventually passed the Federal Safety Appliance Act to create a uniform, national standard.

The Federal Safety Appliance Act requires that railroad companies ensure that certain train/track components and maintenance equipment meet standards that result in a safe environment for workers. This Act is essentially an addendum to FELA. Two of the most important facets of this Act is the requirement of automatic couplers and power brakes which prevent the necessity of workers moving in between train cars. This Act also requires periodic inspections of train car components and maintenance equipment. The failure of railroad companies to abide by the regulations found in this Act can result in federal law violations and civil penalties. Additionally, when a railroad company violates this Act, it creates a negligence per se violation in a FELA suit. "Negligence per se" basically means that the negligence of the defendant has/can be proven by violation of statute. It is a great idea for you as a railroad worker to ensure that you file a FSSA violation in connection with your FELA claim because the railroad company cannot allege contributory negligence as a defense in these cases. Think about it: The railroad company cannot place the blame on the injured railroad worker for failure to provide the proper equipment to do the job.

Railroad company defense: The automatic couplers were improperly set right before the injury to the railroad worker will absolve the company of liability. This is commonly known as the "closed knuckles" defense.

No contributory negligence in appliance cases

Contributory negligence, which goes only to reduce damages in an ordinary FELA case is no defense at all where a violation of the Safety Appliance Act or the Boiler Inspection Act is proved.

Even more important to counsel in such an action is a rule that the plaintiff in such a case need not prove negligence. The United States Supreme Court has repeatedly emphasized that a plaintiff need not prove negligence in situations in which violation of the Safety Appliance Act has resulted in a worker's injury. "a failure of equipment to perform as required by the [FSAA] is in itself an actionable wrong."

No Specific Appliance Defect Needed - Guaranteed Performance

It should be emphasized that a plaintiff is under no obligation to demonstrate a specific defect in an appliance in order for the FSAA to apply. While violation of the Act may be demonstrated through proof of a particular defect, violation of the Act may also be established by showing "a failure to function, when operated with due care, in the normal, natural and usual manner." The equipment used on the job by railroad workers must be guaranteed to perform under normal working conditions.

If your FELA claim occurred as a result of misaligned draw-bars, you need to speak to a FELA attorney immediately. Call my office for a free initial consultation at (832) 458-1756.

Boiler Inspection Act/Federal Locomotive Inspection Act

The Federal Locomotive Inspection Act a.k.a Boiler Inspection Act demands that the locomotive portion of a train be in safe, working condition. Similar to the Federal Safety

Appliance Act (FSAA), a negligence per se standard is established if the locomotive is defective. A violation of this statute serves as proof that the railroad company was negligent in its duties to the employee and you will not have to prove negligence to recovery monetary damages. The locomotive must not possess conditions or defects in the equipment that would endanger the crew.

The BIA/LIA, 49 U.S.C. § 20701, provides:

A railroad carrier may use or allow to be used a locomotive or tender on its railroad line only when the locomotive or tender and its parts and appurtenances— (1) are in proper condition and safe to operate without unnecessary danger of personal injury;

(2)

have been inspected as required under this chapter and regulations prescribed by the Secretary of Transportation under this chapter; and

(3)

can withstand every test prescribed by the Secretary under this chapter.

***Slipping hazard created by foreign substances in a locomotive creates a violation of the Federal Locomotive Inspection Act.

FELA and Railroad Law Tip:

Your injury claim must be filed within three years of when you knew or should have known that you had a work-related injury. Usually, this means the date you got hurt.

Chapter 3: Getting Medical Treatment and Paying Your Medical Bills

Immediate Actions To Take After Injury

Get the union representative involved and present while you are filling out the accident report. Never sign, say, or agree to anything in the report that the claims agent or your supervisor is attempting to force down your throat and that you know is not accurate or a true representation of the events that led to your injury. Put the company on notice in the accident report and preserve the fault of your employer by identifying and defective equipment in the accident report. It is not your fault that you were injured so do not let the company attempt to portray it that way.

Always identify and defective equipment that caused or contributed to your injury.

Feel free to go to your doctor for your treatment. The railroad company is still liable for your medical treatment even if you do not go to the company's preferred physician or hospital. Chances are that if you go to the hospital that the company recommends that the attending physician may attempt to downplay your injuries. It's sad and is not supposed to happen, but in some situations it does.

Here is a quick scenario: Although you were hurting after the coupling of a few cars where your arm was seriously scraped by a misaligned draw-bar, you decided that you would be okay if you took a few aspirin and placed a cold compress on your forearm at home. Feeling a bit sluggish and agitated, you drifted off to bed around 6pm. The alarm clock sounded promptly at 5am and screeching vibrations pulsed through your body. Turning over and pulling your body upright to face the digital demon head on, you quickly realize your body feels like you played an entire NFL game with no pads on. Your neck, back, and legs are throbbing like each body part has its' own heartbeat. You look back at your arm and the laceration has now started to froth and boils surround your cut. The adrenaline that was pumping during the accident has worn off and your body begins to comprehend the extent of your injuries.

This is not the time to try to be Luke Cage or Jessica Jones. Your attempt to hide or ignore your injuries will affect your compensation. Claims agents will view your ignorance of the insurance process as a gap in treatment. This means that they will devalue the monetary value of your claim, allege that you were not hurt, your injuries are not as serious as you later depict, or that you were injured by another source later after the railroad injury. There is a general time-line that you must adhere to regarding your maritime injury to face the path of least resistance from the opposing insurance company. As I have stated before, the insurance company will attempt to thwart your collection of a proper settlement or award by poking holes in your case. Attacking your treatment record is a common occurrence by claims agents and defense lawyers to lower the settlement offers.

Don't Feel Up To Giving A Statement?

The railroad company's representatives cannot attempt to get a statement from you if you have worked more than 12 hours that day.

Railroad Unemployment Insurance Act

The Railroad Unemployment Insurance Act also known as "RUIA" provides benefits for qualifying railroad employees who are seeking assistance in the form of unemployment benefits or sickness/accident benefits. Railroad workers do not receive workers compensation or Social Security. Instead, the Railroad Retirement Board handles the permanent disability and retirement benefits of railroad worker employees. Contact the Railroad Retirement Board when you are considering your long-term benefits at (877) 772-5772.

The first 14 days of unemployment are not paid if it is because the employee is on strike. In order to qualify for benefits under the RUIA, the employee must be willing to work.

Short Term Benefits (Medical and Sickness Benefits)

The railroad claims agent may lie to you and say that you are required to see the company doctor in order to have your medical bills paid. This is a blatant lie and attempt to intimidate you. If you are injured on the job, please go see your own doctor and anyone your doctor recommends. Always seek out the best medical care for your injuries regardless of the medical cost. If the claims agent or insurance carrier is attempting to deny liability for your claim it is because the company is attempting to minimize liability. They hope you will drop the claim even though you are in pain. If you do not attend your medical treatments, this will negatively impact the settlement amount or damage award that you ultimately recover.

In order to qualify for sickness benefits you must be unable to work from your injury or illness. The best way to prove that you cannot work is by having your own doctor state in a letter (statement of sickness) that you are unable to safely perform the task/duties that your job requires. If you are unable to complete Form SI-10, Statement of Authority to Act for Employee, then have your spouse, a trusted friend, or an adult child fill it out for you. The Form SI-10 must have your statement of sickness attached to it when filing for sickness benefits.

You should file for accident benefits as soon as you can. Failure to file your application for sick benefits within the 30 day period window of the date of injury, may result in the Railroad Retirement Board (RRB) not paying for your resulting back-pay of roughly $1500 monthly. In order to qualify in any given benefit year, you must qualify by hitting certain minimum earning requirement during the previous calendar year. Sickness benefits apply not only to your injury, but will cover your maternity needs if you are pregnant at the time of injury as well.

"A day of sickness is a day on which the employee is unable to work because of sickness or injury and for which he or she does not receive any pay and has filed an application for sickness benefits and a statement of sickness. The statement of sickness provides evidence of the employee's medical condition and its expected duration. It must be signed by the employee's doctor (or other authorized individual)."**Source**: Railroad Retirement Board

"As indicated above, a claimant may not receive benefits for any day for which pay is received. This includes railroad and non-railroad wages, salary, pay for time lost, pay while sick, dismissal allowances, most wage guaranty payments, vacation pay, holiday pay, military reservist pay, earnings from self-employment, or remuneration other than subsidiary remuneration. However, payments received under a Railroad Retirement Board-approved nongovernmental supplemental unemployment or sickness insurance plan, an employee's own health or accident insurance policy, or a group insurance policy will not affect entitlement to benefits and should not be reported on claims."**Source**: Railroad Retirement Board

The top medical insurance providers for railroaders nationally are: Aetna, Blue Cross- Blue Shield, and United HealthCare.

Since these benefits are set up exclusively for the railroad worker, he/she cannot "double dip" and receive state or federal benefits outside of these programs while simultaneously getting benefits from the RUIA. Additionally, receiving severance pay will bar you from receiving benefits under RUIA as well.

Long-Term Benefits (Unemployment and Retirement Benefits)

Long-term benefits are principally considered as unemployment or retirement benefits because they will will last much longer in duration. Additionally, these benefits are considered by many facing FELA claims when the employee has been seriously maimed or killed on the job. Never try to handle your long-term benefits completely on your own especially if you are injured. Get your union representative involved. This person is a valuable source in ensuring that you receive everything that is owed to you by way of the company's negligence. Remember, you have a right to choose your own doctor and a right to file a lawsuit against the railroad company that is profiting off your labor and caused your injury.

To qualify for unemployment benefits, you must be willing to work and able to work. You receive this benefit from the Railroad Retirement Board.

"A **qualified employee** is one who earns qualifying creditable compensation in a base year ($3,637.50 in 2016; $3,862.50 in 2017) counting no more than a certain amount in any month ($1,455 in 2016; $1,545 in 2017). In addition, a new employee must have some employment in at least 5 months of the first year worked in the railroad industry in order to draw benefits in the following benefit year.

A *day of unemployment* is a day on which a qualified employee is able to work and available for work and does not receive any pay, is not disqualified, and has properly registered for unemployment benefits. Any calendar day on which the employee does not work solely because of mileage-limitation or work-restriction agreements or solely because he or she is between regularly assigned trips or tours of duty or because a turn in pool service was missed is not considered a day of unemployment. An extra-board employee can receive unemployment benefits between jobs if the miles and/or hours actually worked were less than the equivalent of normal full-time work in his or her class of service during the 14-day claim period. Entitlement to benefits would also depend on earnings." **Source**: Railroad Retirement Board

If for some reason, you do not qualify for annuity benefits or permanent railroad disability after getting injured on the job, feel free to apply for Social Security benefits with Social Security Administration.

Disqualifications for benefits

"A claimant for unemployment benefits may be disqualified for 30 days if he or she refuses to accept suitable work or fails to follow instructions to apply for work or to report to an RRB office or a State unemployment office for an interview.

A claimant who leaves either railroad or non-railroad work voluntarily without good cause is disqualified, starting with the day he or she leaves work, until he or she has returned to railroad employment and earned wages sufficient to qualify for benefits again. This disqualification also applies to a claimant who leaves work voluntarily with good cause, but only with respect to periods in which he or she could receive unemployment benefits under another law.

A claimant is also disqualified for any day on which he or she takes part in a strike begun in violation of the Railway Labor Act or in violation of the established rules and practices of a labor organization of which he or she is a member. This disqualification only applies to claimants who work on the premises where the strike occurs and who do the same kind of work as the employees participating or directly involved in the strike.

An employee who is paid a separation allowance is disqualified for both unemployment and sickness benefits for roughly the period of time it would have taken to earn the amount of the allowance.

A claimant may be disqualified for sickness benefits if he or she fails to take a medical examination when required by the RRB.

If a claimant makes a false or fraudulent statement or claim to obtain unemployment or sickness benefits, he or she will be disqualified for 75 days and may also be subject to a fine or imprisonment. The RRB conducts checks with Federal agencies and all 50 States, the District of Columbia, and Puerto Rico as well as railroads in order to detect fraudulent benefit claims. The RRB also checks with physicians to verify the accuracy of medical statements supporting sickness benefit claims." **Source:** Railroad Retirement Board

Frequently Asked Questions About Annuities and Occupational Disabled

"The Railroad Retirement Act provides disability annuities for railroaders who become totally or occupationally disabled. Medicare coverage before age 65 is also available for totally disabled employees and those suffering from ALS (Amyotrophic Lateral Sclerosis) or chronic kidney disease.

The following questions and answers describe these disability benefits, their requirements, and how to apply for them.

1. How do railroad retirement provisions for total disability and occupational disability differ?

A total disability annuity is based on permanent disability for all employment and is payable at any age to employees with at least 10 years (120 months) of creditable railroad service and, under certain conditions, to employees with five to nine years of creditable railroad service after 1995.

An occupational disability annuity is based on disability for the employee's regular railroad occupation and is payable at age 60 if the employee has 10 years (120 months) of railroad service, or at any age if the employee has at least 20 years (240 months) of service. A current connection with the railroad industry is also required for an occupational disability annuity. The current connection requirement is normally met if the employee worked for a railroad in at least 12 of the 30 months immediately preceding his or her annuity beginning date.

If an employee does not qualify for a current connection on this basis, but has 12 months of service in an earlier 30-month period, he or she may still meet the current connection requirement. This alternative generally applies if the employee did not have any regular employment outside the railroad industry after the end of the last 30-month period which included 12 months of railroad service, and before the month the annuity begins. Full or part-time work for a non-railroad employer in the interval between the end of the last 30-month period including 12 months of railroad service, and the month an employee's annuity begins, can break a current connection.

2. Under what conditions can disabled employees with five to nine years of service be eligible for railroad retirement disability annuities?

Employees with five to nine years of service after 1995 may qualify for an annuity based on total and permanent, but not occupational, disability if they have a disability insured status under social security law. A disability insured status is established when an employee has social security or railroad retirement earnings credits in 20 calendar quarters in a period of 40 consecutive quarters ending in, or after, the quarter in which the disability began.

Unlike the two-tier annuities payable to a 10-year employee, disability annuities payable to five-year employees are initially limited to a tier I social security equivalent benefit; a tier II benefit is not payable in these cases until the employee attains age 62. And, the employee's tier II benefit will be reduced for early retirement in the same manner as the tier II benefit of an employee who retired on the basis of age, rather than disability, at age 62 with less than 30 years of service.

3. How do the standards for total disability and occupational disability differ?

An employee is considered to be totally disabled if medical evidence shows a permanent physical and/or mental impairment preventing the performance of any regular and gainful work. A condition is considered to be permanent if it has lasted, or may be expected to last, for a continuous period of at least 12 months or result in death.

An employee is considered to be occupationally disabled if a physical and/or mental impairment prevents the employee from performing the duties of his or her regular railroad occupation, even though the employee may be able to perform other kinds of work. An employee's regular occupation is generally that particular work he or she has performed for hire in more calendar months, which may or may not be consecutive, than any other work during the last five years; or that work which was performed for hire in at least one-half of all the months, which must be consecutive, in which the employee worked for hire during the last 15 years.

4. How does the amount of a railroad retirement disability annuity compare to a social security disability benefit?

Disabled railroad workers retiring directly from the railroad industry at the end of fiscal year 2014 were awarded almost $2,870 a month on the average, while awards for disabled workers under social security averaged over $1,235.

5. When is early Medicare coverage available for the disabled?

In general, Medicare coverage before age 65 may begin after a disabled employee annuitant has been entitled to monthly benefits based on total disability for at least 24 months and has a disability insured status under social security law. There is no 24-month waiting period for those who have ALS (Amyotrophic Lateral Sclerosis), also known as Lou Gehrig's disease. The fact that an employee is initially awarded an occupational disability annuity does not preclude early Medicare coverage, if the employee's physical and/or mental condition is such that he or she is totally and permanently disabled.

Medicare coverage on the basis of permanent kidney failure requiring dialysis or a kidney transplant is available not only to employee annuitants, but also to employees who have not retired but meet certain minimum service requirements, as well as spouses and dependent children. For those suffering from chronic kidney disease, coverage may begin with the third month after dialysis treatment begins, or earlier under certain conditions.

6. Do the railroad retirement disability annuity requirements include a waiting period similar to the one required for social security disability benefits?

Yes. A five-month waiting period beginning with the month after the month of the disability's onset is required before railroad retirement disability annuity payments can begin. However, an applicant need not wait until this five-month period is over to file for benefits.

The Railroad Retirement Board (RRB) accepts disability applications up to 3 months in advance of an annuity beginning date which allows the agency to complete the processing of most new claims before a person's actual retirement date. An employee can be in compensated service while filing a disability application provided that the compensated service is not active service and terminates within 90 days from the date of filing. When an employee files a disability application while still in compensated service, it will be necessary for the employee to provide a specific ending date of the compensation.

Compensated service includes not only compensation with respect to active service performed by an employee for an employer, but also includes pay for time lost, wage continuation payments, certain employee protection payments and any other payment for which the employee will receive additional creditable service.

7. What documentation is required when filing for a railroad retirement disability annuity?

Employees filing for disability annuities are required to submit medical evidence supporting their claim. Applicants should be prepared to furnish dates of hospitalization, names and dosages of medication, names of doctors, etc. Applicants may also be asked to take special medical examinations given by a doctor named by the RRB. If a disability applicant is receiving workers' compensation or public disability benefits, notice of such payments must be submitted.

Sources of medical evidence for railroad retirement disability purposes may include, but are not limited to, the applicant's railroad employer, personal physician and hospital, the Social Security Administration, or the agency paying workers' compensation or public disability benefits. This evidence generally should not be more than 12 months old. In addition, proof of age and proof of any military service credit claimed and a description of past work activity will also be required.

8. What is the best way to apply for a railroad retirement disability annuity or early Medicare coverage?

Applications for railroad retirement disability annuities are generally filed at one of the RRB's field offices, or at one of the office's Customer Outreach Program (CORP) service locations, or by telephone and mail. However, applications by rail employees for early Medicare coverage on the basis of kidney disease have to be filed with an office of the Social Security Administration, rather than the RRB.

To expedite filing for a railroad retirement disability annuity, disabled employees or a family member should schedule an appointment at the nearest RRB field office. Appointment requests can be submitted to a local RRB office by phone or mail, or by using Field Office Locator to send a secure message. For the appointment, claimants should bring in any medical evidence in their possession and any medical records they can secure from their treating sources, such as their regular physician. Employees who are unable to personally visit an RRB office or meet an RRB representative at a CORP service location may request special assistance, such as having an agency representative come to a hospital or the employee's home. RRB personnel can assist disabled employees with their applications and advise them on how to obtain any additional medical evidence required or any other necessary documents or records.

9. Can an individual continue to receive an employee disability annuity even if he or she does some work after it begins?

Special earnings rules apply to disability annuitants and they are more stringent than those that apply to annuitants who have retired on the basis of age and service. Disability annuities are not payable for any month in which the annuitant earns more than $850 in 2015 in any employment or self-employment, exclusive of work-related expenses. Withheld payments will be restored if earnings for 2015 are less than $10,625 after deduction of disability-related work expenses. Failure to report such earnings could involve a significant penalty charge.

These disability work restrictions cease upon a disabled employee annuitant's attainment of full retirement age (age 65 for those born before 1938 to age 67 for those born in 1960 or later). This transition is effective no earlier than full retirement age, even if the annuitant had 30 years of service. Earnings deductions continue to apply to annuitants working for their last pre-retirement non-railroad employer.

If a disabled annuitant works before full retirement age, this may also raise a question about the possibility of that individual's recovery from disability, regardless of the amount of earnings. Consequently, any earnings must be reported promptly to avoid over payments, which are recoverable by the RRB and may also include penalties.

10. Does employment with a rail labor organization affect eligibility for a disability annuity?

Payment of an employee's disability annuity cannot begin earlier than the day after the employee stops working in compensated service for any railroad employer, including labor organizations. Such work includes service for more than $24.99 in a calendar month to a local lodge or division of a railway labor organization. Also, work by a local lodge or division secretary collecting insurance premiums, regardless of the amount of salary, is railroad work which must be stopped.

11. Must an employee relinquish employment rights in order to receive a disability annuity?

An employee can be in compensated, but non-active, service while filing a disability annuity application as long as the compensated service terminates within 90 days from the date of filing. However, in order for a supplemental annuity to be paid or for an eligible spouse to begin receiving benefits, a disability annuitant under full retirement age must relinquish employment rights." **Source:** Railroad Retirement Board, FAQs

It usually takes around four months or so to start receiving benefits from the Railroad Retirement Board. **If you have questions or concerns about your occupational annuity or disability benefits, you can always call RJ**

Alexander Law, PLLC for a free initial consultation regarding your FELA claim.

Should You Take The Ride To The Emergency Room Via Ambulance?

It depends. Generally, this is a judgment call. If your vehicle did not sustain serious damage and you feel that you can make it to the hospital on your own then you may not want to take the ambulance to the hospital. At this point in the case, the other driver's insurance company has not accepted liability. Even if the other driver states at the scene of the railroad injury that it was "my fault" this does not mean that his insurance company will automatically accept responsibility for the crash. The statement by the driver is a feather in your cap to help prove your case should it have to move forward into litigation. .

You must understand that personal injury litigation is a bit of a gamble for the client and the lawyer. You are assuming that the other party has enough insurance to cover your injuries especially if you did not get coverage beyond liability insurance. The attorney is taking on your case assuming that they can cover your medical bills, provide some sort of financial compensation for your damages, and make a profit for the services that he/she has provided. Ambulance fees have risen over the years so no one wants to incur this fee unless it is necessary.

Caveat: No matter who is at fault in the accident if you are in severe pain then you should allow the paramedics to treat you and take you to the hospital. Unless you are a licensed medical professional (and even then you could be in a state of shock), attempting to self-diagnose yourself when you are injured or feeling this way is a horrible idea. You could have suffered broken ribs, internal bleeding, or a host of other injuries that are not visible to the naked eye. Always err on the side of caution. You only have one body so take care of it.

Should You Go To The Emergency Room Later If You Are Hurting And Did Not Take The Ambulance Ride?

Absolutely. It is imperative that you go seek treatment for your injuries. Many people believe because they were involved in a railroad injury case that they are entitled to a large amount of money from the other party due to inconvenience of having their life interrupted by another's negligent behavior. Negligence is a personal injury tort or cause of action. Negligence is satisfied by identifying four elements that were present at the time of the crash.

Whether you go to the hospital in an ambulance or you decide to drive yourself there later here are the items that you need to document while at the emergency room:

1. Prescriptions and dosages.
2. Name, telephone number, and address of the hospital.
3. Names and contact information (if possible) for ER nurses and treating doctors
4. Telephone number of the hospital medical records department and instructions on how to get the medical records.. This often overlooked, but one of the most important items on this list.

FELA Act and Railroad Law Tip:

Generally speaking, you have three years to file a FELA Act railroad law case. It is a bad idea to wait that long to file a lawsuit. Don't cut it close.

Anytime you are involved in a vehicle crash there is a possibility that you will be injured as a result of someone's negligence. If you are injured on a railroad DO NOT attempt to rush back to work against doctor's orders. You need that time to heal and going back to work before you are fully recovered could actually affect your health in negative, adverse manner. This is especially true as it relates to people who suffer severe injuries.

Losing Job Wages

The most devastating impact of a personal injury is the loss of life. Yet, for those of us who are fortunate enough to survive a railroad injury, trying to restore our lives after a catastrophic injury is just as debilitating. Given the current economic times, many Americans are one paycheck away from financial ruin. Therefore, you need to an effective personal injury lawyer to advocate for you during this tumultuous time in your life. Being confined to your house or the hospital bed means that you are losing wages if you work. Your bills are falling behind. Your mortgage is due.

Relax.

The person who was driving and/or owns the vehicle is responsible for your lost wages and pain and suffering. At RJ Alexander Law, PLLC, we will hold any party accountable for your injury. In any railroad injury case, the plaintiff, you, are entitled to compensation that cover your loss of earning capacity. These damages include your past and future earnings capacity. This is different from the loss of money that you had at the time from your job. Loss of earning capacity means your lower capability to make the same type of money that you made before the car accident. This means that an unemployed, 45 year old make can recover future of earnings capacity damages.

DOCUMENT YOUR LOSS OF EARNING CAPACITY SO THAT YOU CAN HELP YOUR ATTORNEY BUILD THE CASE. CALL

YOUR EMPLOYER'S HUMAN RESOURCES DEPARTMENT AND REQUEST YOUR LASTEST PAYSTUBS.

Paying Your Medical Bills

Typically, you will have already incurred some of sort of medical bills if you are injured by a motor vehicle collision in the form of emergency room, ambulance transport, treating physician, x-ray bills, etc... The good news is that you will not have to pay these bills immediately. The bad news is you will need more treatment and the bill collectors will hound you until you secure a lawyer to help your. Lawyers are able to work with medical professionals to assist you with getting further medical treatment you need by sending out what is called a "letter of protection." This letter of protection tells the medical provider that in the event that the client recovers financial compensation from the at-fault driver's and insurance company that the lawyer will guarantee the provider will be paid. This allows you to seek the physical attention you need in some circumstances to get better.

In other situations, you may have your own health insurance and they may cover the injuries that you sustain.

When your insurance company finds out that there is a lawsuit because of someone's negligence then it may subrogate the medical expenses to the insurance company of the negligent driver.

PURCHASE A DIARY AND KEEP TRACK OF YOUR INJURIES AND HOW YOU ARE FEELING DURING THE RECOVERY PROCESS. INCLUDE THE DATES FOR ANY SIGNIFICANT EVENTS.

Whether you have insurance or not, do not worry about the medical bills so much as about getting better and receiving the treatment you need to get back to a normal life. Hospitals will generally not pester your about the quick payment of your medical bills once your lawyer has contacted them and let them know that your case is currently in litigation.

ALWAYS GET A LETTER FROM YOUR DOCTOR ESTIMATING FUTURE MEDICAL TREATMENT COST AND DURATION OF INJURY.

Types of Doctors and Other Medical Professionals

Acupuncturist- These medical professionals are trained in a traditional Chinese medicine that seeks to improve physical and mental health by stimulating certain points on the body. These acupuncture points serve as stimulation or release areas for the nervous systems and naturally-occurring human hormones.

Anesthesiologist - Anesthesiologists are defined as study the effects and reactions to anesthetic medicines and administer them to a variety of patients with pain-killing needs. They assess illnesses that require this type of treatment and the dosages appropriate for each specific situation.

Chiropractor - Chiropractors focus on the treating neuromuscular disorders through manipulation and manual adjustment of the spine.

Dermatologist - Dermatologists study the structure and function of human skin, They examine patients when auto railroad injury victims have experienced severe road rash or burns.

Emergency Medicine Physician - Emergency Medicine doctors are defined as a medical specialty concerned with the care and treatment of acutely ill or injured patients who need immediate medical attention.

General Practice Physician - General practice doctors as defined as a physician or veterinarian whose practice is not limited to a particular medical specialty.

Orthopedist- Orthopedists deal with the human skeletal system along with broken and fractured bones in railroad injury victims.

Occupational Medicine Physician/Therapist- These medical professionals assist railroad injury victims recover through implementing therapeutic use of everyday activities that the person may find hard to perform after the railroad injury. They help people readjust to life with a severe or permanent injury in the workplace and at home.

Pediatrician- Pediatricians are doctors that focus on infants, children, and adolescent' development, injuries, and diseases that are prevalent in childhood.

Physical Therapist- Physical Therapists are defined as therapy for the preservation, enhancement, or restoration of movement and physical function impaired or threatened by disability, injury, or disease that utilizes therapeutic exercise.

Plastic Surgeon- Plastic surgeons perform cosmetic or superficial surgery to enhance or "correct" physical features of the patient after a significant injury.

Psychiatrist - Psychiatrists study mental and behavioral patterns and processes. The study of psychiatry is a branch of medicine that deals with the science and practice of treating mental, emotional, or behavioral disorders especially those dealing with faulty interpersonal relationships. They will often work with clients on a one-to-one basis to ease mental illnesses and behavioral disorders.

Neurologist - Neurologists work with the human brain to understand the causes, symptoms, and cures for serious and terminal illnesses. Additionally, they study the nervous system and how diseases and injuries may affect the brain and ability to freely move around.

Nurse Practitioner - These medical professionals are nurses who are able to prescribe medicine (Normal registered nurses are unable to prescribe medicine). They can diagnose injuries and treat patients.

Rheumatologist - This physician is trained in the diagnosis and treatment of bones, joints, and muscles. The doctor is usually board-certified in another area of advanced medicine as well.

Common Medical Tests

Magnetic Resonance Imaging (MRI)- A MRI is a 2D or 3D picture of the inside of your body. This test lets doctors see pictures of the inside of your body (muscles, nerves, bones, and other organs such as the gall bladder).

Computerized Tomography Scan (CT/CAT Scan) - This is a 2D (sometimes 3D) imaging test that takes numerous views of the inside of your body to detect clots, tumors, infections, and other diseases and conditions.

X-Rays - X-rays are 2D images of your bones. These images serve as initial surveys of your injuries.

Ultrasound- This 2D type of medical imaging uses reflective sound-waves to diagnose injury. It is used to determine if you suffered internal bleeding as a result of the railroad injury. Additionally, a 3D ultrasound (at least) is always recommended for any pregnant woman involved in a collision to check on the status of her unborn child.

PET Scan - Positron Emission Tomography also known as a "PET" scan is a 3D imaging test that uses radioactive tracers to check for diseases or injuries to the body. The tracers are absorbed by the body. A PET scan is routinely used when dealing with potential brain injuries or problems with the nervous system.

Nerve Conduction Velocity (NCV) - This is a nerve study is also called a "NCV" or Electromyograph (EMG) test. It is used to identify whether nerve destruction exist as a result of the injury. The test measures the speed of conduction of an electrical impulse through a nerve. Victims of serious collisions may discover that they are experiencing numbness in a particular body region. You may be experiencing abnormal pressure from a pinched nerve as a from a herniated or bone fracture/displacement. Shooting sensations or tingling feelings are common symptoms of nerve damage. Common medical terms used to describe conditions resulting from a collision include radiculopathy or neuritis.

Electrocardiogram (EKG) - is a test that shows how the heart is pumping and whether you have suffered an aortic injury. Electrodes are placed on your skin and connected to a machine. The printout will tell the doctor conditions like a heart attack, a heart that beats too slow or fast. More importantly, an EKG can detect a cardiac contusion that results from a vehicle railroad injury. A cardiac contusion is a bruised area of the human heart (aortic injury) caused by blunt trauma to the chest wall or extreme vehicle deceleration. This usually happens your chest wall strikes the steering wheel, vehicle console, interior side panels, or airbags. When you experience injuries to the chest cavity, sternum, or fractured/broken ribs you need to have a EKG test conducted. Common symptoms of cardiac contusions of low blood pressure (hypo-tension) and an irregular heart beat (arrhythmia).

Traumatic Brain Injuries

Traumatic Brain Injuries also known as "TBI" events occur in railroad injury cases when your head strikes an object or your head has been suddenly and violently shaken. Brain injuries have serious, life-long consequences that can go undetected for days, weeks, or even months after a vehicle railroad injury. TBI events can affect your cognitive function and emotional behavior. These injuries may be misdiagnosed or missed by initial emergency treatment room physicians and staff. TBI injuries worsen over time if left untreated. If you have suffered a railroad injury and feel that you have suffered a TBI injury then request that your doctor perform a Positron Emission Tomography (PET) scan or a Single Photon Emission Computerized Tomography (SPECT) scan.

Below are symptoms to Traumatic Brain Injury symptoms (this is not a conclusive list):

1. Persistent Headaches, Seizures, and Vision Issues

2. Inability To Process Information The Same As Before The Railroad Injury, Amnesia

3. Sleep Disorders

4. Depression, Severe Mood Swings, Inability To Control, Altered Personality

5. Nausea or Vomiting

6. Slurred Speech

7. Extreme Sensitivity To Light and Sound

8. Vertigo (Balance Problems), Fatigue

9. Blacking Out At The Scene At The railroad injury Or Afterwards, Fainting, Dizziness

10. Constantly Repeating Phrases or Actions, Short/Long-term Memory Loss

11. Inability To Recognize Pre-Collision Family, Friends, Things, Pets, or Objects

LOSING CONSCIOUSNESS AT THE SCENE OF THE RAILROAD INJURY MEANS YOU HAVE LIKELY EXPERIENCED A SIGNIFICANT TRAMAUTIC BRAIN INJURY. CONTACT RJ ALEXANDER LAW, PLLC IMMEDIATELY AT (832) 458-1756.

How Much Is My Case Worth?

This the million dollar question...the one that everyone wants immediately answered. The short answer is that no one conclusively knows at first. A trained, experienced FELA Act lawyer only really knows how much your case is generally worth until all your body damage is assessed, medical treatment is completed, and compensation sources are identified. *There are a number of variables that accompany this problem including but not limited to:*

1. Insurance Policy Limits

2. Indemnity Clauses (General Contractor and Subcontractor Issues)

3. Did someone die as a result

4. Extent of your provable, medical damages

5. Cost of future medical care (including surgery)

6. Future lost income

7. Charisma (Likability/Personality) of client in front of jury

8. Number of people hurt

FELA and Railroad Law Tip:

Under the Federal Railroad Safety Act ('Whistle blower Law'), 49 U.S.C. Section 20109, you are protected if the railroad attempts to deny, delay or otherwise interfere with your receiving medical treatment if injured at work. To be protected under the law, you must ask to be taken to the hospital.

Chapter 4: Understanding The Claims Process, Your Rights, and Compensation

The first thing you should understand is the Railway Labor Act a.k.a. "RLA." The RLA was originally created in 1926. It provides a system for how railroad worker disputes are handled within the railroad company market. It is essentially the grievance system to handle labor problems between employees (the union) and employers (railroad companies). These issues can range from pay raises, medical benefits, and working conditions (major disputes) to an individual's working hours issue (minor dispute).

Minor disputes are handled by the internal control resolution plan of the particular railroad company. If it cannot be handled in this manner then the employee can go before the Public Law Board or National Railroad Adjustment Board. The Public Law Board is the most common avenue to handle minor disputes and is composed a tribunal. The PLB has a neutral member, a labor official, and a railroad company official. The goal of the tribunal is to determine the correct course of action under the collective bargaining agreement negotiated between the railroad company and the union representatives. Although the PLB decision can be be appealed, the federal court has limited scope of review regarding these decisions.

However, the important thing to understand about PLB minor dispute situations is that these tribunals are not intended to limit recovery of the employee's damage award under a FELA claim. This has been proven by case law that shows PLB tribunals do not grant the same benefits and constitutional rights to that FELA claims were enacted to protect.

<u>You or your lawyer should demand copies of:</u>

1. Human resource manuals
2. Railroad management policy manuals
3. Railroad medical policy manuals
4. Any posted letters or distributed emails that affect or deal with your injury
5. Suspect job offers (a common tactic by railroad companies to lessen your claim)
6. Before/after injury drug test results

7. Names and other information of persons who apply and receive job offers for same jobs you have been offered or rejected for

8. Railroad rehabilitation programs

9. Names and other information of other persons who have faced similar injuries as you.

Occupational Diseases

Like many other blue-collar jobs, working for railroads is a hard job. The work is strenuous and forces employees to work long hours under dangerous conditions. More importantly, working in these types of conditions can expose you to various illnesses that may not reveal themselves until much later in your railroading career or during retirement. Occupational diseases are brought about by encountering a number of accumulative, dangerous conditions on your job. For example, in many construction, rail-yard, and ship dock jobs; hearing loss tends to be a huge problem that creeps up on the unsuspecting rail-yard worker because you do not lose your hearing in one feel swoop. Rather, the constant, daily noise of the brakes, horns, and trains deteriorate your hearing over time. The constant exposure to the crashing cars along with other loud noises will cause you to lose hearing over time and it usually takes ten years or so to register the loss.

Your railroad employer likely requires you to participate in a yearly hearing loss test that will alert you to a possible hearing loss claim. Keep in mind that the statute of limitations on your FELA claim begins to run when you know or SHOULD KNOW that you have a potential FELA claim. If you suspect that you have a hearing loss claim then you need to schedule an appointment with an audiologist because you have three years to file suit on this FELA claim. Even if you wear earplugs or ear muffs on the job, you still have a potential FELA claim against any railroad company that has employed you.

Here is a listing of common causes of occupational diseases/illnesses

1. Climatic conditions - exposure to extreme heat and cold
2. Overexertion
3. Exposure to toxic fume inhalation/chemicals
4. Aggravated pre-existing condition
5. Highway-rail collision/impact

6. On track equipment impact

7. Repetitive motions

8. Assaulted by a co-worker

9. Collisions between on track equipment

10. Exposure to poisonous plants

11. Rubbed or abraded equipment

12. Bitten/stung by Animal/Insect

13. Slipped, fell, or stumbled on track equipment

14. Derailment

15. Lost Balance

16. Blowing/Falling debris

17. Caught between track equipment

When an occupational disease such as cancer makes an employee fear for his/her life or experience extreme terror as a result of contracting it, the Supreme Court has ruled that mental anguish damages are available when it is confirmed that the railroad employee contracted it as a result of working for railroad company. I have not included every single occupational disease simply because there are too many to mention, but **if you believe that you have suffered an occupational disease** as a result of working for a railroad company feel free to **call RJ Alexander Law, PLLC anytime at (832) 458-1756.**

Below I have listed the things you should and should not do when it comes to handling your accident report/claim. As I stated earlier, if there are violations with your equipment then you do not have to prove negligence under your FELA claim.

Should

1. Identify all coworkers/onlookers who witnessed the injury take place. Get their contact information immediately. When the time comes for your attorney to contact these parties it will help to significantly reduce the time that it takes to properly assess their value to your case.

1. Always inform your union representative. Immediately.

1. Your attorney needs to take the statements of any coworkers/onlookers. If you know these people them tell them that your attorney will need to do this. It prepares them to not feel so uncomfortable with the

pressure surrounding the case. They should willing to cooperate by fully disclosing any information they have because they know this is helping their friend and coworker.

1. Try to hire your attorney as soon as possible. The longer that you wait, the more time passes and memories and facts become cloudy.

1. Know the Internal Control Plan for your railroad company as it relates to medical and accident reports. If you fail to timely complete these forms then the company may attempt to use this against you in the PLB hearing or argue that you didn't attempt to mitigate your damages in your FELA claim.

1. When you get to your doctor and when you feel out any accident report: do not hold back on detailing each and every place you feel pain. These forms will eventually be examined by the railroad's attorney and the claim agent. You need to inform these people how this accident has affected you and if you hold back on fully

detailing your injuries then the company will hold back when it comes to fully compensating you.

1. Document everything and keep a journal. Keep any paperwork you receive whether it is a prescription, bill, receipt, etc...

Should Not

1. Never sign ANY documents without consulting with your attorney!

1. Never sign any medical releases/HIPPA forms/authorizations with consulting with your attorney!

1. Never pay a personal injury attorney for an initial consultation on your FELA claim.

1. Do not depend on the railroad company doctor for sound medical advice. This is the equivalent of getting a concussion in a NFL football and asking the team doctor whether he thinks it is safe for you to go back in the

game. Spend the money on your own doctor if you have to.

1. Never give a statement to the claim agent or any representative of the railroad company without first consulting your union representative and legal counsel.

Failed Drug/Alcohol Test Situations

A railroad company drug test that adhere to the Federal Railroad Administration standard is a failed (positive) test only when it is verified by a medical review officer and the employer is notified or when the test results in a positive drug test for any Schedule I-V drug and the employer will defend the test results in a court of law.

Railroad companies are required to report failed drug tests to the FRA's Office of Railroad Safety and the National Response Center.

Obviously, you cannot be under the influence of drugs while performing your job unless you have been prescribed medicine by a physician or other medical professional who is aware of your job duties and authorizes it. If you fail a drug test then you need to ensure that you preserve your medical prescriptions.

Below are the conditions needed to prevail in a failed drug test situation as an railroad employee:

(1)

The treating medical practitioner or a physician designated by the railroad has made a good faith judgment, with notice of the employee's assigned duties and on the basis of the available medical history, that use of the substance by the employee at the prescribed or authorized dosage level is consistent with the safe performance of the employee's duties;

(2)

The substance is used at the dosage prescribed or authorized; and

(3)

In the event the employee is being treated by more than one medical practitioner, at least one treating medical practitioner has been informed of all medications authorized or prescribed and has determined that use of the medications is consistent with the safe performance of the employee's duties (and the employee has observed any restrictions imposed with respect to use of the medications in combination). (b) This sub-part does not restrict any discretion available to the railroad to require that employees notify the railroad of therapeutic drug use to obtain prior approval for such use. 49 CFR 219.103

A railroad company cannot allow you to return to work after injury without a medical certification from a physician on file that KNOWS what your job entails and agrees that is is safe for you to return to work.

FRA will provide copies of accident/incident reports under the Freedom of Information Act (FOIA) upon written request. Written requests for copies of accident/incident reports should be accompanied by the appropriate fee and addressed to:

Freedom of Information Act Coordinator
Office of Chief Counsel
Federal Railroad Administration
U.S. Department of Transportation
RCC-10, Mail Stop 10

West Building 3rd Floor, Room W33-437

1200 New Jersey Avenue, SE.

Washington, DC 20590

Accident/Incident Record-keeping and Reporting Requirements

Reportable accidents/incidents are divided into three major groups for reporting purposes. These groups correspond to different FRA forms and are as follows:

1. Group I – Highway-rail grade crossing accident/incident (Form FRA F 6180.57)
Note: For highway-rail grade crossing accidents/incidents only, railroads are required to
contact potentially injured highway users involved in a highway-rail accident/incident, by
mail, using a Highway User Injury Inquiry Form record (Form FRA F 6180.150) and, if
unsuccessful, by phone. The Form FRA F 6180.150 shall be sent with a cover letter
drafted in accordance with the requirements set forth in the FRA Guide and a

preaddressed, prepaid return envelope. Railroads are to use the information gathered to
comply with FRA's accident/incident reporting and recording requirements.

2. Group II – Rail equipment accident/incident (Form FRA F 6180.54)

Note: Accident reports citing an employee human factor as a cause must be accompanied by an Employee Human Factor Attachment (Form FRA F 6180.81). In addition, each implicated employee must be provided with a Notice to Railroad Employee Involved in Rail Equipment Accident/Incident Attributed to Employee Human Factor (Form FRA F 6180.78).

Note: In preparing a rail equipment accident/incident report, the railroad must inquire
into the possible involvement of alcohol/drug use or impairment and report such
information to FRA as required by § 225.18.

3. Group III – Death, injury, or occupational illness (Form FRA F 6180.55a)

In preparing a Form FRA F 6180.55a for a fatality involving a trespasser, the

railroad is responsible for acquiring additional documentation with regard to cause of

death. **Source:** U.S. Department of Transportation

Late, Amended, and Updated Reports

Late Reports. When a railroad finds that an accident/incident was omitted from a previous month's submission, a completed report and a letter explaining the reason for the late filing are to be sent to FRA. The late report and letter are to be forwarded no later than the next monthly filing.

Late reports are not to be attached to or included in counts of reports prepared for the current month. Any late report is to be filed for the year and month in which the original event occurred.

Take, for example, the following scenario: An employee sustains a minor injury in June, but none of the reporting criteria are satisfied. He or she is reexamined in July because of complications and is instructed to take prescription medication and remain off work for 3 days. In this instance, a late report for the month of June must be prepared.

Amended Reports. When a railroad discovers that an accident/incident has been improperly reported on a previous month's submission, then an amended report must be submitted to FRA with a letter of explanation. The amended report and letter are to be forwarded no later than the next monthly filing. The report should have the notation "Amended Report" at the top of the form, and items being changed are to be circled in red. **Source:** U.S. Department of Transportation

OSHA Whistle blower (Federal Railroad Safety Act)

The Federal Railroad Safety Act was created to protect employees who inform the government that their railroad employer is violating the law.

Covered Employees

Under FRSA, an employee of a railroad carrier or a contractor or subcontractor is protected from retaliation for reporting certain safety and security violations. Protected Activity If your employer is covered under FRSA, it may not discharge you or in any other manner retaliate against you because you provided information to, caused information to be provided to, or assisted in an investigation by a federal regulatory or law enforcement agency, a member or committee of Congress, or your company about an alleged violation of federal laws and regulations related to railroad safety and security, or about gross fraud, waste or abuse of funds intended for railroad safety or security. Your employer may not discharge or in any other manner retaliate against you because you filed, caused to be filed, participated in, or assisted in a proceeding under one of these laws or regulations. In addition, you are protected from retaliation for reporting hazardous safety or security conditions, reporting a work-related injury or illness, refusing to work under certain conditions, or refusing to authorize the use of any safety- or security-related equipment, track or structures. You may also be covered if you were perceived as having engaged in the activities described above. In addition, you are also protected from retaliation (including being brought up on charges in a disciplinary proceeding) or threatened retaliation for

Such actions may include:

• Firing or laying off

• Blacklisting

• Demoting

• Denying overtime or promotion

• Disciplining

• Denying benefits

• Failing to hire or rehire

• Intimidation

• Making threats

• Reassignment affecting promotion prospects

• Reducing pay or hours

• Disciplining an employee for requesting medical or first-aid treatment

• Disciplining an employee for following orders or a treatment plan of a treating physician

• Forcing an employee to work against medical advice

How to File a Complaint

A worker, or his or her representative, who believes that he or she has been retaliated against in violation of this statute may file a complaint with OSHA. The complaint should be filed with the OSHA office responsible for enforcement activities in the geographic area where the worker lives or was employed, but may be filed with any OSHA officer or employee.

Whistle blower Protection for Railroad Workers

Individuals working for railroad carriers are protected from retaliation for reporting potential safety or security violations to their employers or to the government.

- Boston (617) 565-9860

- New York (212) 337-2378

- Philadelphia (215) 861-4900

- Atlanta (404) 562-2300

- Chicago (312) 353-2220

- Dallas (972) 850-4145

- Kansas City (816) 283-8745

- Denver (720) 264-6550

- San Francisco (415) 625-2547

• Seattle (206) 553-5930

Addresses, fax numbers and other contact information for these offices can be found on the Whistle blower Protection Programs website, www.whistleblowers.gov, and in local directories. Complaints may be filed orally or in writing, by mail (we recommend certified mail), e-mail, fax, or hand-delivery during business hours. The date of postmark, delivery to a third party carrier, fax, email, phone call, or hand-delivery is considered the date filed. If the worker or his or her representative is unable to file the complaint in English, OSHA will accept the complaint in any language. Results of the Investigation If the evidence supports your claim of retaliation and a settlement cannot be reached, OSHA will issue a preliminary order requiring the appropriate relief to make you whole.

Ordered relief may include:

• Reinstatement with the same seniority and benefits.
• Payment of back-pay with interest.
• Compensatory damages, including compensation for special damages, expert witness fees and reasonable attorney's fees.

• Punitive damages of up to $250,000. OSHA's findings and preliminary order become a final order of the Secretary of Labor, unless a party objects within 30 days. Hearings and Review After OSHA issues its findings and preliminary order, either party may request a hearing before an administrative law judge of the U.S. Department of Labor. A party may seek review of the administrative law judge's decision and order before the Department's Administrative Review Board.

Deadline for filing complaint

Complaints must be filed within 180 days after the alleged adverse action occurred.

Under FRSA, if there is no final order issued by the Secretary of Labor within 210 days after the filing of the complaint, then you may be able to file a civil action in the appropriate U.S. district court.

Source: Occupational Health Safety and Administration Fact Sheet

If the railroad company that you work for is self-insured then you should contact a FELA attorney immediately. Do not try to handle a matter like this on your own.

FELA and Railroad Law Tip:

Unlike worker's compensation, under the FELA you must prove the railroad's negligence caused your injury or you are not entitled to receive compensation for your injury. Under FELA, the fact that you are injured while working for the railroad DOES NOT mean you are entitled to a claim for damages against the railroad for your personal injury.

Chapter 5: Railroad Civilian Injuries

In an ideal world, there would never be serious injuries or fatalities between trains and automobiles. Indeed, some city planners have argued that trains and automobiles should never meet because railroads should either be built above or below street level. Someone in an automobile is more than 20 times more likely to die in a collision with a train than any other motor vehicle. In 2016, there were 2,025 train collision at highway-grade crossings, 2655 fatalities, and 798 injuries. Generally, highway-grade crossing accidents have declined over the years, however, even one train collision with an automobile is too much. More people still perish from car-train collision than all U.S. aviation crashes.

A collision between a train and car is similar to car running over a soda can. You should always be careful when attempting to cross a railroad-grade crossing because a train will not be able to stop if you become stuck on it. The driver is usually aware of the impending train collision before the train conductor because the railroad crossing arms alert you to the oncoming train, the average train weighs 12 million pounds, and the distance that a train needs to stop is generally at least one mile. You are essentially playing with your life if you attempt to go around or ignore the warning signals that a train is coming.

If you are involved in a railroad grade-crossing accident, it may not be apparent to you who is liable or who to sue for compensation. You need to contact a personal injury lawyer that focuses on railroad grade crossing cases. Otherwise, you stand to leave the mediation table or courtroom unsatisfied with the result. Generally speaking, the railroad company would be the main culprit who you would want to pursue if you are involved with this type of collision and it was not your fault that the situation occurred.

When you are dealing with a railroad-grade crossing case, your goal is to show the jury that the railroad's negligent behavior caused your injuries. Now the negligence of the railroad company can take many forms and the actions of the railroad employees can best demonstrate the negligent behavior of the company itself. In the event of a railroad-grade crossing there are at least three employees on the train whose actions should be heavily scrutinized by your train accident lawyer, they are the:

1. Brakeman - is responsible for watching for vehicle attempting to cross railroad crossings. Basically, he is the guy who alerts the conductor to the fact that they are about to hit.
2. Conductor - is responsible for the speed of the train, sounding the horn, applying emergency brakes in the event of a looking collision, looking out for vehicle on the tracks at railroad crossings, and listening to other crew members for warnings of a collision.
3. Roadmaster - is responsible for the upkeep of the railroad grade crossing.

***There are a number of other parties who could be responsible for your injuries. Do not accept any sort of settlement, no matter how huge or enticing, until a lawyer who actually handles railroad-grade crossings examines your case and identifies all potential, liable parties.**

The four major reasons for civilian railroad crossing accidents are: crossing conditions, sight obstructions, train speed and whistles, and inadequate protections.

Crossing Conditions

Crossing gates are inspected at least once a month as required by federal law. Many states have created laws that give railroad companies a duty to alert drivers to oncoming trains. The laws may slightly vary and they may be pre-empted by federal law if there is one that substantively covers the issue at hand. Most of the time, the railroad tracks are owned by the railroad company traversing them.

Sight Obstructions

The most common sight obstruction in railroad grade crossing accidents is vegetation on or near the railroad tracks. It is possible that this may bring another possible defendant into the lawsuit if the railroad was not responsible for the surrounding area where the injuries occurred. Most states have some sort of law dealing with vegetation around railroad track.

Train Speed and Whistles

The average train is traveling somewhere around 35 mph when the automobile and train collide at railroad grade crossings. This speed is still fast enough to kill you and any occupants in your vehicle. "Since their inception, railroads have sounded locomotive horns or whistles in advance of grade crossings and under other circumstances as a universal safety precaution. During the 20th century, nearly every state in the nation enacted laws requiring railroads to do so. Some states allowed local communities to create 'whistle bans' where the train horn was not routinely sounded. In accordance with a statutory mandate, FRA issued regulations which took effect in 2005 that require locomotive horns be sounded in advance of all public highway-rail crossings, and provide local communities the option of silencing them by establishing quiet zones. Under the Federal regulation, locomotive engineers must sound train horns for a minimum of 15 seconds, and a maximum of 20 seconds, in advance of all public grade crossings, except:

• If a train is traveling faster than 45mph, engineers do not have to sound the horn until it is within ¼ mile of the crossing, even if the advance warning is less than 15 seconds.

• If a train stops in close proximity to a crossing, the horn does not have to be sounded when the train begins to move again.

• A "good faith" exception at locations where engineers can't precisely estimate their arrival at a crossing. Wherever feasible, train horns must be sounded in a standardized pattern of 2 long, 1 short and 1 long and the horn must continue to sound until the lead locomotive or train car occupies the grade crossing. The minimum volume level for locomotive horns is 96 decibels and the maximum volume level is 110 decibels. Establishing a Quiet Zone Only local governments or public agencies may establish a quiet zone, which must be at least ½ mile in length, and have at least one public highway-rail grade crossing. Every public grade crossing in a quiet zone must be equipped at minimum with the standard or conventional automatic warning devices (i.e. flashing lights and gates).

Communities have the option to establish partial quiet zones restricting locomotive horn sounding during overnight hour's between 10:00 P.M. to 7:00 A.M. Local governments must work in cooperation with the railroad that owns the track, and the appropriate state transportation authority to convene a diagnostic team to assess the risk of collision at each grade crossing where they wish to silence the horn. An objective determination is made about where and what type of additional safety engineering improvements are necessary to effectively reduce the risk associated with silencing the horns based on localized conditions such as highway traffic volumes, train traffic volumes, the accident history and physical characteristics of the crossing, including existing safety measures." **Source:** Federal Railroad Administration Locomotive Horn Sounding and Quiet Zone Establishment Fact Sheet

Inadequate Protections

The state, county, or city government may be responsible for the collision if they are responsible for maintaining the safety control devices that alert drivers to oncoming trains. If the crossing arms or warning lights fail to activate then you may have a potential suit against the manufacturer of that particular equipment.

I won't go into detail about federal pre-emption because we covered that in the first chapters of the book. I'll suffice it to say that this area of law is very nuanced and requires a specialist to handle. Recent court cases have attempted to define when a federal law applies to civilian railroad-grade crossing cases and preempts state law claims (unsafe speed cases and railroad warning device cases must apply federal law). Of course, railroad companies like the idea of taking every case such as this to federal court because the state law may vary somewhat in how negligence is proven and the eventual outcome of the case could be more plaintiff-friendly in some jurisdictions versus others. As stated before, it is possible that your case may have to be heard in federal court because the Federal Railroad Safety Act (FRA) preempts your state's personal injury laws.

49 U.S.C. § 20106 (2000) (formerly 45 U.S.C. § 434) of the FRSA provides: "Laws, regulations, and orders related to railroad safety and laws, regulations, and orders related to railroad security shall be nationally uniform to the extent practicable. A State may adopt or continue in force a law, regulation, or order related to railroad safety or security until the Secretary of Transportation (with respect to railroad safety matters), or the Secretary of Homeland Security (with respect to railroad security matters), proscribes a regulation or issues an order covering the subject matter of the state requirement. A State may adopt or continue in force an

additional or more stringent law, regulation, or order related to railroad safety or security when the law, regulation, or order— (1) is necessary to eliminate or reduce an essentially local safety or security hazard; (2) is not incompatible with a law, regulation, or order of the United States government; and (3) does not unreasonably burden interstate commerce." Part one is considered the exception to federal law pre-emption. It is commonly known as the "local hazard" rule. It is a way for civilian railroad-grade crossings to apply state law in the face of a FRSA or any other federal law that would preempt it.

Definitions

Highway-Rail Grade Crossing Accident/Incident. Any impact between on-track railroad equipment and a highway user at a highway-rail grade crossing.

Highway-rail grade crossing means:

(1)

a location where a public highway, road, or street, or a private roadway, including associated sidewalks, crosses one or more railroad tracks at grade; or

(2) a location where a pathway explicitly authorized by a public authority or a railroad carrier that is dedicated for the use of non-vehicular traffic, including pedestrians, bicyclists, and others, that is not associated with a public highway, road, or street, or a private roadway, crosses one or more railroad tracks at grade. The term "sidewalk" means that portion of a street between the curb line, or the lateral line of a roadway, and the adjacent property line or, on easements of private property, that portion of a street that is paved or improved and intended for use by pedestrians. The term "highway user" includes automobiles, buses, trucks, motorcycles, bicycles, farm vehicles, pedestrians, and all other modes of surface transportation motorized and un-motorized. All crossing locations within industry and rail-yards, ports, and dock areas are considered highway-rail grade crossings within the meaning of the term.

Obstruction Accident. An accident/incident in which a consist strikes: 1) a bumping post or a foreign object on the track right-of-way; 2) a highway vehicle at a location other than a highway-rail grade crossing site; 3) derailed equipment; or 4) a track motorcar or similar work equipment not equipped with AAR couplers and not operating under train rules.

Explosion-Detonation. An accident/incident caused by the detonation of material carried or transported by rail. A detonation occurs when a shock wave exceeds the speed of sound.
Explosions-detonations resulting from mishaps during loading or unloading operations, and those caused by fire aboard on-track equipment, are included in this definition.

Fire or Violent Rupture. An accident/incident caused by combustion or violent release of material carried by or transported by rail. Examples of this type include fuel and electrical equipment fires, crankcase explosions, and violent releases of liquefied petroleum gas or anhydrous ammonia.

Other Impacts. An accident/incident, not classified as a collision, that involves contact
between on-track equipment. Generally, these involve single cars or cuts of cars that are damaged during switching, train makeup, setting out, etc., operations. If both consists contain a

locomotive, an EMU locomotive, or a DMU locomotive, the event should be classified as a collision between trains.

Sources of Definitions: *U.S. Department of Transportation*

Below I have included a checklist of things to get at the scene when hit by a train:

Train Crew Information:

- Name/Title

- Address

- DOB

- Telephone

- Locomotive engineer certificate information (State driver license not required to be in possession of engineer or recorded on accident report).

Train Information:

- Lead locomotive number

- Train ID or symbol assigned by the railroad

- Number of cars in the train

- Initial and number of railroad car stopped on crossing

- Owner of tracks (name & address)

- Railroad company operating train (name & address)

- Train stopping distance from point of impact

Ask Crew Member to Operate Locomotive Safety Devices:

- Headlight and auxiliary lights

- Horn (CAUTION - Horn is Loud)

- Locomotive Bell

Crossing Information (Take pictures of all below):

- Crossbuck Sign

- Multiple Track Sign

- Advance Warning Sign

- Pavement Markings

- Active Warning Devices functioning

- DOT crossing inventory number

- Distance from Advance Warning Sign to nearest rail

- Crossing surface

- Visual obstructions (vegetation, structures, etc.)

FELA and Railroad Law Tip:

The federal "train horn" rule requires that locomotive horns be sounded at public highway-rail crossings and provides flexibility to localities to silence horns.

Chapter 6: Damages For Personal Injuries Not Resulting In Death

Damages You Can Recover For A FELA Claim

FELA damages won't differ according to the state where the injury occurs. The federal government has established a uniform standard when it comes to determining your damages. Under FELA, a plaintiff can recover damages for past and present pain and suffering, unpaid medical expenses, lost earnings, loss of earning capacity, and emotional-distress.

Railroad Worker Damages

The damages a railroad worker can receive as a result of his/her injuries are:

1. past and future pain
2. Loss of enjoyment of life
3. Past and future medical expenses
4. Emotional distress
5. Nature and extent of the injury

6. Loss of earnings in the past and future or loss of earning ability

7. Fringe benefits (three years worth of medical-dental-vision insurance coverage)

You may only recover for emotional distress when you are actually in the zone of danger. The zone of danger refers basically to the area where the injury occurred. The question to ask yourself when contemplating whether you were in the zone of danger is: could I have been injured by the negligent act that transpired? This situation is applicable whether you are discussing a particular physical injury such as an equipment-caused amputation or the potential infection of a disease such as silicosis or asbestos.

Tier I and II taxes should not be subtracted from the computation of your FELA claim. Consult your FELA attorney for more information.

When future damages is awarded, interest collects on the damages award from the time it is paid until the point when the future damage (benefit) would be expected/received.

FELA and Railroad Law Fact:

The train accident rate in 2016 was the lowest in history and down 42 percent from 2000; the employee injury rate in 2016 was down 46 percent from 2000; and the grade crossing collision rate in 2016 was down 39 percent from 2000. By all of these measures, recent years have been the safest in rail history. The train derailment rate, the train collision rate, and the rate of accidents caused by defective track were the lowest ever in 2016.

Railroad Track Classifications - Class I, Class II, and Class III freight railroads?

Class I Railroad – a freight railroad with an operating revenue exceeding $457.9 million. Seven Class I freight railroads operate in the United States: Burlington Northern Santa Fe Railway, CSX Transportation, Grand Trunk Corporation, Kansas City Southern Railway, Norfolk Southern Combined Railroad Subsidiaries, Soo Line Corporation, and Union Pacific Railroad. Canadian National Railway and Canadian Pacific Railway are also considered Class I due to their significant trackage in the United States.

Class II Railroad – often called a "regional railroad." Class II railroads have operating revenues between $36.6 million and $457.9 million.

Class III Railroad – often called a "short line railroad." Class III railroads have operating revenues of $36.6 million or less. **Source:** Surface Transportation Railroad

FELA and Railroad Law Tip:

The amount of money an injured railroad worker is entitled to recover is decided by two factors: how serious his injuries and losses are, and whether he can show that his injury was in some way, or in some part, due to the fault of the railroad, the negligence of any of its employees, or some defect in equipment, tools, or any unsafe working condition.

Chapter 6: Wrongful Death and Survival Actions

Death cases are truly traumatic events that require the proper time and attention to each detail of the case. If your loved one has died while employed on a railroad, you need to hire an attorney as soon as possible. Do not attempt to handle a matter like this alone.

These wrongful death cases are not based on the ability to continue or pursue a lawsuit on behalf of the deceased, but creates a cause of individual action for the beneficiary because of the lost he/she has sustained through the loss of the decedent (deceased person).

Federal Employers' Liability Act wrongful death lawsuits are presented by a personal representative for the benefit of a surviving spouse and children, for the decedent's parents, or, the dependent next of kin -- in that order of preference. Damages in FELA wrongful death lawsuits are controlled by federal law; not state law, so a state's wrongful death act will not apply in the event of a railroad worker's FELA case.

In a wrongful death action under FELA, the deceased employee's representative/beneficiary is entitled to:

(1) the present value of financial contributions that the deceased (decedent) would reasonably be expected to have given his/her family had he/she lived;

- Lost financial contributions can include the entire remaining life expectancy of the decedent even when he/she could have expected to retire at an earlier age.

(2) the pecuniary value of services which the spouse might reasonably have expected to receive from the decedent in the future; and

- A pecuniary loss revolves around some sort of reasonable expectation of assistance, benefit, and/or support from the decedent...and that the spouse or child had been deprived of this assistance, benefit, and/or support.

- Monetary awards are computed based on the present cash value of any future benefits, assistance, and/or support.

- The jury can consider the type of person the decedent was in order to determine the value that he/she would have provided for his/her family.

- The jury can consider income sources that are not related to the railroad worker's employment.

(3) the loss to his/her children during their childhoods of the training, nurture, education and guidance of their father/mother.

(4)

conscious pain and suffering of the decedent prior to death.

- Emotional pain and suffering and mental anguish damages can be awarded for the pain the decedent faced before his/her death.

- These damages revolve around the initial time of injury until death and can be heightened by the anxiety or fright that the worker (decedent) may have experienced even in the few seconds before his/her imminent death.

FELA has never described what exactly is "negligence." It has also never stated exactly what should guide the jury in computing a monetary award amount for the spouse or children left behind as a result of railroad worker's wrongful death.

Adult children of the deceased can recover monetary damages when they had a "reasonable expectation" that the pecuniary contributions of the decedent would have continued beyond the age of 17 and into adulthood.

If someone you know or love is injured and you believe a third party may be partly responsible for their demise, then you need to contact a lawyer immediately. Only a skilled lawyer familiar with this area of law will be able to determine whether the state premises liability law will apply or FELA.

Railroad Wrongful Death Civilian Cases

Understand that states vary according to how they treat wrongful death cases and it is possible for a civilian to pursue a lawsuit in federal court depending on the activities of the railroad company. I have included Texas law as a preview of some sorts for those who would want to pursue a cause of action as a civilian in state district courts. You should consult an attorney in these matters and not attempt to handle them yourself.

Texas State Law

Understanding Wrongful Death Actions

Damages in a personal injury cause of action can include a variety of expenses especially so when someone had died as a result of someone's negligence. Normally, you are suing someone for the damage to your body in the way of scarring and disfigurement, medical expenses, loss wages from work, and injuries sustained to your physical property. In unfortunate cases where your loved one has perished as the result of someone's act or omission regarding his/her operation of a vehicle or negligent entrustment of a vehicle, there are more remedies available to you.

Elements of a Wrongful Death Claim:

1. The plaintiff is a statutory beneficiary of the decedent;
2. The defendant is a person or corporation;
3. The defendant's wrongful act causes the death of the decedent;
4. The deceased person (decedent) could file a lawsuit if he/she had lived and;

5. The victim (plaintiff) actually suffered an injury.

What does this mean to you?

Texas Wrongful Death Act

The Texas Wrongful Death Act, was created for the surviving spouse, children, and parents of someone killed to recover for the resulting damages experienced as the result of the person's death (decedent).

1.   The plaintiff is a statutory beneficiary of the decedent.

The person who files the lawsuit must be by law a spouse, child, or parent of the deceased person. The marriage to the decedent can be by formal or informal (common-law) marriage, but there are specific items that you must satisfy in order to meet either requirement. Additionally, there exists certain measures that must be taken by someone in a common-law marriage with the decedent after their death to prove that the marriage was valid. Wrongful death actions operate in a similar function to probate cases in this manner, in that an executor or administrator of the estate can be identified as the statutory beneficiary who can bring a wrongful death action against the defendant vehicle owner.

Same sex couples can legally bring a wrongful death action against the defendant vehicle owner. Biological children, legally recognized adopted children, parents, adult children, legally recognized adoptive parent, and divorced parents can all file successful lawsuits on the behalf of their parents or children. Stepparents, foster parents, and grandparents CANNOT bring a suit for the wrongful death of stepchildren, foster kids, or grandchildren.

IN SOME SITUATIONS, YOU CAN FILE A LAWSUIT FOR A CHILD BORN DEAD THAT DIED AS THE RESULT OF A railroad INJURY CASE. DO NOT TRY TO HANDLE THIS TYPE OF CASE ALONE.

2.   The defendant is a person or corporation.

Under the Texas Wrongful Death Act, this is a pretty simple concept to understand, the defendant has to be a human being or some form of business. Satisfying this element can get pretty tricky when you are dealing with any form of government entity or employee because sovereign immunity allows the governmental entity to block liability for responsibility in some instances. It has been repeated many times over, but you should contact a lawyer and not try to handle a case of this size on your own. The statute of limitations to notify governmental units is often much shorter than the general, two year, personal injury statute of limitations and the requirements for notifications can be difficult to obtain and understand without the proper legal knowledge.

3.   The defendant's wrongful act causes the death of the decedent

In wrongful death suits there is generally an underlying cause of action that is alleged in the lawsuit (petition). Whatever the initial (underlying) cause of action is attempting to prove must show that this action caused the death of the decedent.

THERE ARE MANY DEFENSES THAT A WRONGDOER WILL ATTEMPT TO USE TO GET OUT OF LIABILITY. TWO OF THE MOST WIDELY USED ARE THAT THE VICTIM (DECEDENT)

WAS SOMEHOW AT FAULT OR THAT ANOTHER PERSON
CAUSED THE ACCIDENT.

4. The deceased person (decedent) could file a lawsuit if he/she had lived

If the railroad injury victim had lived then he/she would have been able to bring a lawsuit for his/her injuries. Anything that would apply to the cause of action for the decedent if he/she was alive would also fall on the cause of action for the statutory beneficiary as well.

5. The victim (plaintiff) actually suffered an injury.

One of the major differences between a wrongful death action versus a survival one is that the statutory beneficiary, plaintiff, in the wrongful death lawsuit is the person who has to prove damages that he/she suffered as the result of the victim dying. In a survival action, it is about the injuries that the victim suffered.

<u>Compensation</u>

The types of damages available to under a Texas Wrongful Death Action include:

Actual Damages - damages awarded to the plaintiff to compensate for harm or injury. *These include:*

> **1. Pecuniary (Economic) Losses** - loss of services, care, earning capacity, maintenance, etc...from the deceased.

> **2. Mental Anguish** - mental harm or torment that the plaintiff experienced as a result of the loss of railroad injury victim.

> **3. Loss of Companionship** - damages driven by love, relationship, and comfort lost as a result of victim's death.

> **4. Loss of Inheritance** - damages driven by what the plaintiff would have received from victim if he/she had lived a normal life span and died a natural death.

Exemplary Damages - These are expenses that are available when the victim's death is caused by the gross negligence or willful act/omission (failure to act) by the defendant driver/owner of the vehicle.

A. **Interest** - from the time the injury occurred (ore-judgment) or interest after the verdict (post-judgment).

B. **Attorney Fees**

C. **Court Costs**

FUNERAL EXPENSES ARE NOT RECOVERABLE UNDER A WRONGFUL DEATH ACTION, BUT ARE RECOVERABLE UNDER A SURVIVAL ACTION CAUSE OF ACTION.

Statute of Limitations in a Wrongful Death Action

The statute of limitations for a wrongful death suit involves two claims, as mentioned before, the underlying cause of action and the wrongful death claim itself. The underlying cause of action must be filed within the statutory two year period. Failure to file a lawsuit on this matter will cause both the underlying claim and the wrongful death claim to be permanently barred. The wrongful death claim statute of limitations grants the statutory beneficiary two years from the time of death of the decedent to file a lawsuit.

Survival Death Actions

Survival plaintiffs recover damages for the injuries suffered by the decedent.

Under the Texas Survival Statute, an heir or representation of an estate is allowed to pursue the decedent's personal injury lawsuit. The Statute does not create a new cause of action; it permits the decedent's cause of action to continue after his/her death.

The elements of a survival cause of action are:

1. The plaintiff is the legally recognized representative of the person who died as from the vehicle collision.

2. The deceased person has a cause of action for personal injury to his/her health, reputation, or person BEFORE death.

3. The deceased person would have been able to file a lawsuit if he/she has lived.

4. The defendant vehicle owner/driver's act or omission to act caused the deceased person's injury.

What does this mean to you?

The elements of a survival cause of action are:

1. The plaintiff is the legally recognized representative of the person who died as from the vehicle collision.

In a survival action, the deceased person must be born alive. This is different from the wrongful death action. If the injury involves a child that dies after birth a survival action can be pursued even if the injurious act (vehicle collision) occurred while the child was still inside the mother. A personal representative has to plead in the lawsuit that he/she is the able to bring the lawsuit on behalf of the decedent. An heir must prove that the he/she has the legal right to pursue a survival cause of action. This area of the survival action deals with probate law or the recognition of one's heirs and property and the division and administering of assets by Texas statute or will. Wrongful death actions in Texas can be very complicated because they often involve the intersection of Texas personal injury and probate law. Seek a lawyer as soon as possible if dealing with such a matter.

BIT OF PROBATE LAW: TO DIE WITH A WILL IN PLACE MEANS THAT YOU DIE "TESTATE." DYING WITHOUT A WILL MEANS THAT YOU DIE "INTESTATE."

2. The deceased person has a cause of action for personal injury to his/her health, reputation, or person BEFORE death.

If the deceased had an underlying cause of action for personal injury that existed before he/she perished that stemmed from the vehicle collision injury then a survival action can be lodged against the defendant. The lawsuit can be filed even if the deceased person did not file the personal injury lawsuit before death. If the deceased person did file the lawsuit before death then the lawsuit may be continued by the heir or personal representative.

3.   The deceased person would have been able to file a lawsuit if he/she has lived.

The person who died would have a underlying viable lawsuit to pursue if he/she was alive today.

4.   The defendant's act or omission to act (failure to act) caused the deceased person's injury.

If the defendant's actions cause the death of a person then it satisfies this element.

Compensation

The types of damages available to under a Texas Survival Statute Action include:

Actual Damages - damages awarded to the plaintiff to compensate for harm or injury. In a survival action, the plaintiff can recover damages on the underlying claim as well as the survival action. *These include:*

Pain & Mental Anguish - damages recoverable when the deceased person is aware that he/she is going to die.

Medical Expenses

Funeral Expenses

Exemplary Damages - These are expenses that are available when the victim's death is caused by the gross negligence or willful act/omission (failure to act) by the defendant driver/owner of the vehicle. *These include:*

Interest - from the time the injury occurred (pre-judgment) or interest after the verdict (post-judgment).

Attorney Fees

Court Costs

The statute of limitations in a survival action mirror that of the wrongful death cause of action: If the underlying claim is barred then the survival action will also suffer the same fate.

FELA and Railroad Law Tip:

Collisions at grade crossings, along with incidents involving trespassers on railroad rights-of-way, are critical safety problems. They typically account for well over 90 percent of rail-related fatalities.

Chapter 7: What Should I Look For When I Hire A Railroad Injury Lawyer

The initial occurrence that takes place in the FELA claim process is the actual railroad injury, filing the proper accident forms, and preservation of evidence. A claims agent will contact you and immediately start to figure out how they can minimize your injuries or at least the cost of them for the railroad company. As discussed earlier, the agent will attempt to settle the claim as soon and cheaply as possible. Your FELA claim is driven by proven damages meaning you cannot expect to collect much financial compensation for injuries if you have never sought medical treatment.

If your injuries are not of a catastrophic nature then you will usually have a medical examination completed by a doctor that will diagnose your injuries. Typical injuries from soft tissue injury cases involve your neck, back, knees, legs, and arms. You will then seek treatment with a physician, chiropractor, or other medical professional. Obviously, if the injuries are of a catastrophic nature then you will have already begun treatment and may still be in the middle of it while the case is underway.

FELA and Railroad Law Fact:

Get a copy of anything ANYONE ask you to sign.

At the completion of your medical treatment, your lawyer will submit a settlement demand to the insurance company. A typical railroad injury case can take somewhere from six months to two years to complete depending on the type of injuries involved, the willingness of the at-fault driver's insurance to cooperate and settle the case, and backlog of cases on court's docket if the case does have to go to trial.

Purpose of Initial Consultation

When you are deciding to meet with a personal injury attorney, you will need to discuss a plethora of things with him/her. Railroad injury case consultations can be quite lengthy due to the general severity of the injuries. They boil down to making sure that a proper fact-finding inquiry was initiated. You need to have certain items to ensure that your case is properly processed.

You need to tell your lawyer the truth about your collision. There is nothing worse than withholding information from the very person who is supposed to help you. Withholding information often leads to an adverse verdict or lower settlement. You will want to decide the case facts, how you will pay for your medical costs, injuries you are experiencing, your representation agreement, and legal fees along with the extra costs.

Items You Should Take To The Initial Consultation:

1. Any Medical Treatment Records

2. Medical Prescriptions

3. Phone Numbers and Addresses of Medical Providers and Facilities

4. Witness Information: Names, Phone Numbers, Addresses

5. Police Report

6. Union Hall Contact Information

7. Copy Of Any Filed Accident Reports Signed or Filed on Your Behalf

8. Railroad Insurance Information: Policy Number, Insurance Company, and Claims agent Number/Company Contact Number (if available)

9. Date of the Injury

10. Ownership Information For All Railroads Involving Your Injury

11. Other Injured Persons Information: Names, Phone Numbers, Addresses

12. Rough Sketch of Scene, Showing Position of Train, Cars, Equipment, and Other Details

13. Your Insurance Information: Policy Number, Insurance Company, and Claims agent Number/Company Contact Number

14. Your Human Resource Officer's Name, Number, and Any Other Contact Information

15. Video and/or Photos Of Any And All Vehicles, People, and Objects Involved In The Railroad Injury

Things to Consider During Your Initial Consultation:

1. Do Not Share Information About Your Case On Social Media.

2. Did You Give A Written Or Recorded Statement To The Claims Agent?

3. You Need To Disclose Any And All Insurance Coverage To Your Attorney.

4. Do Not Discuss Your Case With Other People.

Power of Attorney and HIPPA forms

Your personal injury attorney will want to discuss your Power of Attorney agreement. The Power of Attorney agreement will allow the attorney to legally work on your behalf when dealing with the insurance company and any other adverse parties. You will need to sign a HIPPA form. HIPPA stands for Health Insurance Portability and Accountability Act of 1996 (HIPAA). HIPAA is the federal law that establishes standards for the privacy and security of health information.The HIPPA form must be signed by you in order for your attorney to get any medical records that you do not already have in your possession.

Understanding Legal Fees and Contingency Fees

You need to sign a Retainer Contract/Agreement For Representation. If you have questions about the contract then you should definitely read it before you sign. I often tell people to take the contract home with them and if they have any further questions we can discuss it when they return. Legal fees are often higher for personal injury situations because they differ from other areas of legal practice. Family law cases often require you to pay a retainer fee to start working on the case and then an hourly fee once that retainer is extinguished. Criminal law cases may require a retainer as well but you generally know the process of dealing with a criminal case will proceed with pre-trial settings, a trial and then an appeal if needed. So, many criminal lawyers will charge you a flat fee for each phase of a criminal case.

Personal injury lawsuits are handled by contingency fee agreements. Contingency fee agreements means, "I do not get paid as a lawyer unless I collect some sort of financial gain for you." These lawyers generally put up the money to buy your medical records, file your lawsuit, and any other costs associated with processing your case. You need to ask whether you have to pay any fees if you lose the case or decide to go with another lawyer. Because the lawyer is taking a huge risk by investing his/her time, energy, and money into your case with no upfront payment, contingency fee agreement are higher than other legal practice areas. The typical railroad injury case contingency fee ranges somewhere between 33-45 percent depending on the work involved.

If You Decide To Go With Another Lawyer And The Personal Injury Attorney Has Spent Money On Your Case, He/She May Be Reluctant to Release His/Her Interest In The Case. Carefully Choose Your Lawyer Before Signing The Retainer Agreement.

Choosing A Lawyer

You need someone who is willing to fight for you. Choosing a lawyer is a very important aspect of your case because it can dictate the outcome of your financial settlement. The lawyer that you choose should be someone who will be honest and extremely cost-effective. Too many railroad injury victims are hit with expenses in the case that skyrocket the law firm's payment and leaves the injured person with very little money in the end. Some lawyers state that the person must be board-certified and have certain credentials, but **what you need is someone who is not afraid to take your case to trial and can effectively handle him/herself in the courtroom**. It doesn't matter whether the lawyer is 60 years old or 30. Look for the lawyer that understands the insurance claims process and will effectively advocate on your behalf. Below are certain attributes that you should look for in any great personal injury attorney:

1.   *Reputation*

Before you visit the lawyer for the initial consultation do some online research about him/her. What do the reviews say about the lawyer? What does the website look like? Does he/she actually focus on personal injury law or is it a general practice firm? Personal injury law is a very complex area of law and someone who is handling wills, family law, real estate, immigration, and whatever comes through the door may not have the time to devote to your case. Go the your potential lawyer's State Bar website and look up the lawyer. Have there been malpractice claims, license suspensions, or formal complaints successfully filed against the attorney? Has the lawyer written any books on the subject? Spoken at conventions on the subject? What qualifies him/her as an expert on the subject of FELA law? Has he/she handled these types of cases before? What was the outcome?

2. *Will He/She Take The Case To Trial?*

There exists three worlds in personal injury law. First, there are lawyers who advertise for railroad injury cases and refer them to another law firm to handle the actual work. Second, there are lawyers who actually do the work and suck at advertising. Third, there are lawyers who advertise and also do the work. If you can you should bypass the first two types of lawyers because you will spend a good amount of time jumping back and forth between the referral law firm and the one who actually handles your case trying to get answers about what is going on. Sometimes, it is not a bad idea to have your family, friends (who actually know what they are talking about), or trusted lawyer refer your case to another attorney if you already have a relationship with another attorney and they know someone who focuses on the particular type of need that you have. Yet, if you are searching for a lawyer and do not know any attorneys then you should go to the law firm that can handle your case from beginning to end. It makes the situation easier to deal with when you have questions or inquiries about case updates and you can call on your lawyer. More importantly, you need to take your case to someone who is willing to take your case to trial. If the attorney is afraid of going into a courtroom and talking to a jury about your injuries and the damages that you have suffered then how can he/she effectively represent you?

3. Comfort Level & Vibe

Do you feel comfortable with the lawyer? You need to be able to disclose confidential information to this person and release your medical records to him/her. When you have an open and honest relationship with the attorney, you will likely have an easier time achieving your goal of financial and medical compensation.

4. Attorney Responsiveness

FELA cases are not overnight payouts. These cases take time to mature and you need time to heal. Thus, you will need to keep your attorney abreast of any type of medical treatment and pains you are experiencing as a result of the crash. You do not want an attorney working your case that you can never reach. Many attorneys may be willing to meet you initially and talk about your case at first glance, but never return phone calls once you have signed up with a firm. Worst yet, your case may be referred to a "case manager" who is inattentive to your case and does not respond to you in a timely manner when you have questions about your case.

Your case is important and you deserve respect, time, and attention. While most lawyers are busy during the day, you should be able to have an open line of communication with your lawyer and have your emails and phone calls returned in a timely manner.

RJ Alexander Law, PLLC - Standard of Excellence

My firm makes it a habit to return phone calls within a 24 hour period and update clients about their cases every two weeks, if not each Friday. However, this is not a normal practice in law firms. You will be lucky to speak to an attorney about your case once a month if you are lucky. More than likely, you're case will be handed off to a case manager (not a lawyer and probably not a paralegal) who will hopefully handle contact you and keep you informed about your case status. I invite clients to call me and let me know how their medical treatments are going as well. An open line of communication is always important in these types of matters. **Potential client tip:** *Call the lawyer a day or so after the consultation and see how quickly they follow up. If he/she is too*

*busy to return your phone call within a day or so then you
should look elsewhere for legal representation.*

5.   Fee Structure

I have already discussed the contingency fee agreement above. You need to make certain that you understand the fee agreement and any expenses that may occur along the way. Filing court fees, serving the defendant, and printing costs are often additional items that are included in the final calculation of legal fees.

When the case is resolved, the personal injury lawyer will receive the check for your damages. The medical providers and facilities will be paid first and any other bills that resulted from the handling of your case. The attorney will be paid according to your contractual agreement and then you will receive the amount leftover. The typical personal injury lawyer is paid by the client by means of a contingency fee contract. Are you familiar with the commercials where lawyers say, "We don't get paid if you don't get paid."? Well, that is the essence of what a contingency contract is. A personal injury lawyer collecting his/her fee is based on securing the client's money from the negligent party (tortfeasor) and what actions the lawyer must take to achieve the end result.

Because a personal injury lawyer often puts a considerable amount of his/her own money into a case, the fees are higher than typical fee models in other areas of legal practice. For instance, a criminal lawyer may charge you a flat fee for handling specific phases of a criminal case (pre-trial, trial, and/or appellate phase). Personal injury lawyers will charge you a contingency fee that will generally range somewhere between 33 to 45 percent of the amount recovered. If you are a member of a union and this is a FELA case then the contingency fee may be 25 percent.

What Is My Case Worth?

Prospective clients want you to quote them an estimate of how much money they will collect as a result of the auto accident. Cases differ concerning how much each one will pay the injured victim because no FELA/railroad injury is exactly like another.

Who Pays Your Medical Bills?

Your medical bills are paid at the conclusion of your case. This will either happen after a successful trial verdict or accepting a settlement offer.

What Are Liens?

A lien is a court ordered document that allows a third party to place a debt upon a party or person's personal/business property. When dealing with personal injury matters, the third party must place the owing party on notice via the local judicial civil court system.

Hospital Lien - A hospital lien is defined asa cause of action or claim of an individual who receives hospital services for injuries caused by an accident that is attributed to the negligence of another person. For example, in Texas, for the lien to attach, the individual must be admitted to a hospital not later than 72 hours after the accident. The lien extends to both the admitting hospital and a hospital to which the individual is transferred for treatment of the same injury. Tex. Prop. Code §55.002.

Many hospital liens result from people suffering from railroad injury cases. If you did not pay for the services provided at the time of admission or your health insurance did not cover the injuries then you will receive a bill very soon. The lien must be filed with the local county clerk before the settlement is disbursed.

Dealing with liens is a very complicated matter. You should consult with a personal injury attorney if you are dealing with a hospital lien because there are likely more bills or liens lurking around. If you attempt to handle this matter yourself and you prematurely settle your claim you will may face a host of problems. Don't try to save a few dollars thinking that you can handle a serious matter that others have went to school for seven plus years to understand.

Five bills that are usually attached to your hospital visit:

1. Ambulance Transport
2. Emergency Room
3. Physician
4. Radiology
5. Laboratory/Specimen

These bills will sit in a sort of limbo until you resolve your personal injury lawsuit. This bothers some people because they may still receive bills from the providers or hospital while the case is going through the motions toward resolution. You need to understand that these bills will be paid by your personal injury settlement or jury award after taking the case to trial. A typical FELA case time-line ranges somewhere between six months to three years. However, a lawsuit can last years. The at-fault driver's insurance company will usually make you a one-time, lump sum settlement offer that will satisfy your entire bodily injury claim. When you do not know the full extent of your loss then it is very foolish to rush the lawyer to "get you some money now." If you rush this part of your case, it is very likely you miss a bill or expense. Be patient.

Healthcare Provider Lien

So you went to the chiropractor, physical therapist, or physician for injuries resulting from your railroad injury and have not paid your bill? This is not uncommon as many people do not have the funds to pay for health insurance. Sometimes, you do have health insurance, but it will not cover all your medical bills. Remember earlier in the book when we discussed the Letter of Protection that attorneys issue to chiropractors? Well, this serves as a "lien" against your personal injury settlement. Generally, your lawyer will be able to negotiate this amount with the healthcare provider to ensure everyone is paid that provided you services if the settlement amount is not a large amount.

Health Insurance Carrier Lien

Pete Seeger once said, "education is when you read the fine print. Experience is what you get when you don't." Some health insurance carrier plans have fine print language that allows your insurance to claim a medical lien on a injury settlement for the insured.

Medicare and Medicaid Liens

The Medicare Secondary Payor Act (MSP) gives the federal government a statutory lien for any disbursed Medicare payments. If you have worker's compensation or another insurance plan then you may not be responsible for paying Medicare, but you need to consult with a personal injury attorney for help handling this matter.

When a person has Medicaid and it has paid for medical treatment then the state is required to seek payment. Medicaid liens only revolve around the particular payments made treating your damages.

So you have a situation where you suffered a railroad injury and you have called all over town trying to find a lawyer to help you, but everyone keeps turning you down. Well, there are a number of reasons why this might happen. Lawyers who are putting their own money into cases have to be picky about who they chose to represent. It may be because you botched the case without knowing it or it could be because they are already have a full case load. However, it probably boils down to the fact that your case fits into one the categories listed below:

1. *You Are Trying To Sue Someone Prominent In The Community*

Society likes to portray lawyers as blood-thirsty, ambulance chasers who will do anything for a dollar, but the reality is that the vast majority of lawyers are an ethical bunch who are not willing to put their families and livelihoods in jeopardy for a quick dollar. There may be someone in your community who is a prominent, well-liked celebrity or powerful political figure who has injured you. Some lawyers may be reluctant to sue that person because they might know them or are afraid of the potential long-term consequences to their legal career. If you have this problem, the best idea is to contact lawyers in other cities who are do not have the potential conflicts weighing on them.

2. *There are Liability Issues With Your Case*

In personal injury and tort matters when someone refers to liability issues what he/she is stating is that there are problem identifying who is at fault in the railroad injury case. Lawyers who practice railroad injury law can examine a case at the initial consultation and identify liability issues. A seasoned lawyer understands that if he/she spots unusual problems with the liability part of your case then a jury will likely find issues with assigning blame to the other party and in turn compensating your for sustained injuries.

Prime examples of liability issues are when traffic citations are given to you and not the alleged at-fault driver or you were breaking the law while driving such as driving drunk, or all the witnesses who no ties or interest to the parties in the case cite you as the at-fault responsible driver in the collision.

163

3. There is No Insurance Or Assets Available To Compensate You

What happens when the other driver is clearly at-fault but has no insurance, no assets, and no way to compensate you for injuries? Plain and simple: You are screwed. No lawyer is going to take a case. It just isn't going to happen...***UNLESS you have UM/UIM insurance***. Remember that your uninsured and under-insured insurance coverage will help you in these types of situations. This is why it is so important to talk with your insurance agent before an accident and make sure that you are actually "fully covered" in the event of a collision. Filing a lawsuit and taking a case to trial are huge wastes of an attorney's time if it there is no way to assure the client that you will receive some sort of financial compensation.

4. There Are Questionable Or Damage Issues With Your Case

What happens when liability and insurance is no problem, but you have no suffered any severe injuries? A lawyer will likely reject your case. FELA cases are usually serious injury cases. Even cases that involve minimal or cosmetic damage to your railroad or equipment can have significant effects on your body. However, if you have not sought treatment for your cases or are unwilling to do so then this will nullify your chances of compensation. Damages are needed to prove your case. You may need to pursue the case in small claims court if you do not have a few thousand dollars in medical bills. You will be leaving money on the table if you do not seek proper medical care.

FELA and Railroad Law Tip:

A railroad lawyer can handle a car accident case, but not vice versa. FELA lawyers know the FELA law that uniquely protects you. There are so many details, special traps, special rules that can be used to your benefit. The right lawyer will even tell you when you don't need their help.

Chapter 8: Letting A Jury Decide: Taking The Case To Trial

Filing A FELA Lawsuit

    1. Alert the railroad company that you have legal counsel.

    2. Alert any and all medical providers that you have legal counsel.

    3. Alert the railroad by certified letter and email that you have legal counsel.

    4. Revoke all medical access/HIPPA forms/authorizations to your records.

Filing a Lawsuit - Complaint and Answer

    The reality is that some cases must go to trial. When you reach an impasse with the insurance defense lawyer and litigation claims agent, you must take your plea for compensation to the people. ,I love civil litigation and the thrill of talking to a jury. But, the process can be burdensome, cost-prohibitive, time consuming, and anxiety-ridden for the motor vehicle victim (plaintiff). You need to understand that a motor vehicle collision case can take two years to get to trial and sometimes longer, and you need an effective advocate who is familiar with the courtroom.

A complaint or original petition starts your case. It identifies your cause of action, applicable law, damages you incurred, persons or entities that are responsible for your injuries, and the compensation that you are seeking. The defendant(s) will respond with an answer to your complaint.

Depositions

A deposition is is part of the discovery process (finding, gathering, and submitting evidence to the court). Depositions are out-of-court sworn testimony of lawsuit parties or witnesses. They can be used at the time of trial and are employed by plaintiff personal injury lawyers and defendant insurance counsel to assess the case. Many cases are resolved after this point. A transcript of what is said during the deposition is produced and they are also videotaped. The formality of the event often intimidates motor vehicle victims and it is recommended that you speak with your attorney about what happens in the deposition process before it occurs.

The insurance defense counsel will ask questions during the deposition to attack your case viability.

*Below are many **personal character attack** excuses that are usually made by insurance defense counsel:*

1. Your prior criminal record, DWI convictions.

2. Prior driving record,regularity of traffic violations, citations, and convictions.

3. Bringing up any history of documented mental or institutionalized emotional-based problems

4. History of prior collision cases and the outcome

5. Job problems, specifically, failing drug tests.

*Below are a list of excuses used by insurance companies to argue against your **medical diagnosis, treatment, and injuries** in the deposition:*

1. You did not leave the scene of the collision in an ambulance or life-flight transport.

2. You did not go immediately to the Emergency Room after the collision/injury.

3. Your initial pain complaints to the Emergency Room doctor are not the same pain complaints you are seeking follow-up treatment for now.

4. Your primary physician records of complaint do not match the Emergency Room physician records.

5. An Independent Medical Examination (IME) conducted by a recommended insurance company doctor revealed no injuries or pain. IME's are used by insurance company hired doctors to create reports that support the company's view of your pain and suffering.

6. You have missed several physician, therapy, and/or chiropractic appointments.

7. There are numerous medical treatment gaps in your record.

Legal Advising of Union Members

Many attorneys make approach you about wishing to represent you or your loved one in the railroad injury lawsuit or FELA claim. These cases are very difficult and can be easily lost by an attorney who does not specialize in this area of law. Unions select and recommend railroad injury attorneys to represent their members to provide competent legal advice and counsel in these events. Usually, these lawyers provide the union with discounted legal services as a result. The average personal injury lawyer will often charge as much as 45 to 50 percent of whatever they are able to collect. Additionally, states cannot attempt to interrupt the right of lawyers to advocate on behalf of their railroad injury clients in state courts according to Supreme Court precedent.

Jury versus Bench Trials

There are a few differences in jury and bench trials. In a jury trial, the judge serves as the finder of law determining whether questions about law and civil procedure brought forth by the two parties (plaintiff and defendant) are correct. You will routinely hear judges overruling or sustaining objections made by the two opposing parties at trial.　　Additionally, judges will any rule on motions and evidentiary questions during the discovery/pre-trial process. The jury resolves issues of fact and applies the judge's findings of fact meaning that they will listen to your case and determine which side they believe and portion out fault in the collision along with compensation. The jury is selected from members of the local community. In a bench trial, the judge serves both roles (finder of law and finder of fact) and there is no jury.

Jury Size

Jury trials in state district court cases are composed of 12 jurors. Jury trials in county and justice of the peace courts are composed of 6 jurors. Civil trials need 5/6 (five-sixths or 10 of 12) of the jurors to agree with one another to reach a legally recognized verdict.

Opening Statement

All civil cases start by both lawyers (plaintiff and defendant representation) presenting initial statements to the jury. The lawyers provide an overview of the case, claims or defenses that will be employed, significant issues to watch and listen for, and what they are seeking from the jury in the way of compensation.

Presentation Evidence

The lawyers will present any and all evidence about the case to the jury. Evidence is identified by exhibit number or lettering. Evidence is usually admitted before the trial, but may also be presented to the court and admitted now. The jury is allowed to take the exhibits into jury deliberations at the conclusion of the closing statement to further review when making a decision.

Closing Argument

This is the final chance for each side to persuade each juror. A closing argument is a summation of all facts, evidence, and logic that convinces the jury why your client should prevail.

Jury Instructions & Verdict

When the parties have concluded their closing arguments, the judge will provide the jury with a set of instructions that tell them how to employ federal laws. Once the jury reviews all the evidence, the jury will review the instructions to determine who was at fault, the percentage of fault, and how much the plaintiff is owed. The jury verdict will be read by the jury foreman/woman to the court.

FELA and Railroad Law Tip:

Any decision to accept a settlement and give up your right to a verdict must be made carefully. (Here's why you don't want to settle your claim too quickly.) But do not confuse tunnel vision for a verdict with making the smart play in every case.

BONUS CONTENT:
Chapter 9: I Tried To Handle The Case Myself, But I Am In Over My Head

It is a near certainty that there will be some people who pick up this book and read it after attempting to handle their railroad injury situations alone. This chapter is written for you. When the liability of an employer defendant is questioned and you cannot prove that the employer caused the railroad injury, it is possible that the insurance company will deny your claim. If you are going to fight for what is yours and not allow yourself to be taken advantage of by corporate forces then you need to hire a FELA injury lawyer. There is too much that can be lost because you decide to take the high road and not pursue your claim with the help of a railroad injury attorney. Remember, the insurance company and at-fault driver will have and claims agents and lawyers fighting to ensure that you receive as little as possible. Don't go into battle with a stick when what you need is a shield and sword.

Look, the reality of Texas railroad law is that it is becoming more convoluted and hard to deal with daily...even for lawyers who routinely practice personal injury law. So if you do not have the requisite knowledge and time to handle the railroad injury claims process then it makes perfect sense to hire a FELA lawyer. Below are some the instances when you should definitely hire a railroad injury lawyer:

1. Pursuing Multiple Defendants

When there are many defendants involved in a FELA injury case you need to hire a lawyer that focuses on railroad collision law because one or more parties may be responsible for the sustained injuries. Railroad workers will sign releases that will allow the negligent party to walk away from liability because they believe another party was at fault or they do not want to rock the boat on their job.

ONCE YOU SIGN YOUR NAME ON THE DOTTED LINE RELEASING A PARTY FROM LIABILITY THAT CONTRACT AGREEMENT WILL BAR YOU FROM SEEKING ANY COMPENSATION UPON YOUR AGREED AMOUNT.

2.   Permanent Disability

When you have experienced a permanent loss of a limb or function of your brain's cognitive and/or motor skills you should immediately hire an attorney to represent your interests. You will have to live with this debilitating impairment for the rest of your life. A personal injury will know how to measure this injury and demand proper compensation from the wrongdoer. I cannot stress enough that you reach out to a FELA attorney for assistance in this type of matter. You may be experiencing depression or feel insecure about your appearance. It is imperative that you contact a lawyer to preserve the three year statute of limitations and ensure that you seek the proper medical attention you need.

Chances are that if you know someone who has suffered a severe brain or spinal cord injury then he/she may need your help seeking a personal injury attorney. The lawyer will want to make sure that you understand that he/she represents the injured party, not you. When there are serious medical conditions such as a ruptured discs or fractured bones involved in your case then you definitely should hire a personal injury lawyer. These injuries will affect you for the rest of your life. Ask any former runner or college athlete how their joints feel when it rains and you will soon realize that your need to get all the medical attention and financial compensation possible for your sustained damages. A permanent disability is grounds for a larger insurance claim and you will need the expertise of a seasoned lawyer to ensure proper payment.

3.   Wrongful Death Matters

Railroad injury fatalities are unexpected, traumatic events that no one should have to endure. Unfortunately, these situations occur sometimes even when you drive as safely as possible due to the negligence of others on the road. I have a dedicated a chapter to survival and wrongful death cases. I highly recommend that you review that chapter if your loved one has died as a result of a railroad injury.

4.   The Claims agent Has Made You A Firm Low-Ball Offer

If the claims agent has made you a low settlement offer on your case and will not deviate from that amount you need to contact a personal injury attorney. At the very least, you need to seek a consultation to discuss the offer. An experienced railroad injury attorney can be tell you whether this is a fair amount and if he/she can help you recover a larger amount. Sometimes, a lawsuit will need to be filed and you will have to wait longer for a resolution, but this is better than settling the case prematurely for a nominal amount.

5.   Insurance Claim Has Been Denied

When your insurance claim is denied the at-fault driver's representation is telling you from the outset that they have no intention to pay you. In these situations, you must have a lawyer represent you because the only thing that will make an insurance claim back off this stance is the lawsuit filed against its' insured. The insurance company has a duty to defend the insured at-fault driver.

6.   Unaware of the Statute of Limitations In Your Case

If you are unaware of the statute of the limitations in your case then you need to seek the assistance of FELA attorney because if the statute of limitations passes without a filed lawsuit then you will lose the potential to recover for your injuries. Don't expect the claims agent to keep you informed about your case. Remember, the agent does not represent you and is completely adverse to your financial interest.

7.   Complex Claim Involving Heavy Equipment, Materials, or Cargo

Heavy equipment claims usually involve serious injuries because of the size of the items involved. Railroad collision injuries involve larger insurance policies to compensate for the damage they can cause to victims. Also, there are federal laws that govern the transportation of certain types of cargo. FELA claimants suffer significant injuries when dealing with heavy equipment and the coupling/uncoupling train cars. When there are significant injuries sustained, you must retain a railroad injury attorney.

FELA and Railroad Law Tip:

You have 180 days to file a Whistle blower claim against your railroad employer with the Department of Labor. Filing a Whistle blower claim after the 180 period, forever bars you from pursuing this claim.

Chapter 10: Common Insurance Defense Tactics And Mistakes To Avoid

The reality of getting injured on the job is that no one wants to be in this particular situation. You took this job because it offered good pay and a steady way for you to be able to take care of your family. Any experienced personal injury lawyer can tell you that employers may want to do the right thing by you and ensure that you're taking care of by the company. However, this is not always the case in insurance companies today routinely make it increasingly difficult for injured railroad workers to secure proper financial compensation for their injuries. Similar to car wreck victims, injured railroad workers may be placed in a situation where they are unable to return to work or have the ability to financially maintain their lifestyles.The railroad's insurance defense team may also attempt to offer you a small settlement amount in order to quickly resolve the matter and wipe their hands clean of your situation. If you cannot return to work or even worse you are fired later as a result of your inability to properly perform on the job, you will likely regret settling for pennies on the dollar. It is essential that when you are involved in a FELA case that you seek proper legal representation in such matters. My firm is available around the clock to assist you. **Call 832-458-1756 now or email me at rja@rjalexanderlaw.com to schedule your free consultation.**

Common Excuses Used By Insurance Companies To Devalue Your Claim

I've told you before that insurance companies and their employees are not your friends, but it bears repeating. They are constantly working to minimizing your claim because insurance is now a business that concerned with shareholder value and stock prices. They do not care about your injuries. The effective mantra of all insurance companies today is to delay paying you, deny your claim if they can, and defend their reasons of minimizing your claim at all costs. **Railroad claims agents will not alert you to the problems with your case.**

Below are common insurance company tactics used to devalue FELA claims:

1.   **You Refused To Give Or Sign A Statement** - It's sad to say, but insurance claims agents do take into account how old you are when considering what they will pay you for a claim.

2.   **Injury Not Immediately Reported To The Supervisor** - This will not prevent you from pursuing an injury claim, but could certainly lessen the settlement amount that the claims agent is willing to pay you. Potentially, your comparative fault (blame) in the railroad injury increases and thereby reduces causation by the true at-fault railroad company along with the value of your claim.

3.   **Past/Pre-Existing Injury** - Oftentimes, when someone is involved in a railroad injury, he/she may require surgery. Insurance companies blame degenerative changes, congenital, or postural abnormalities as the reasons that people suffer back and neck pain after railroad injuries occur. Claim agents try to make it seem as if the underlying condition already existed before the collision and so they are not responsible for the injury. You are entitled compensation for new injuries and aggravation of medical conditions/past injuries in Texas personal injury cases.

4.   **Medical Treatment Gap** - One thing that I try to stress to every client that walks into my office is that you need to attend

all the recommended medical treatment sessions. If the doctor tells you to do a certain activity to fill better then you should do it. The treating doctor is the person who is most familiar with your type of injury and how to reduce the pain. Additionally, the insurance company's claim agent will lower the settlement offer on your case if there is inconsistent or large gaps in medical treatment. Sometimes, you cannot help missing occasional treatments due to the complications of life and the pain you may be experiencing due to the your injuries. However, if you completely halt your medical treatment and resume it, the insurance company will try to halt payment for your treatment on the last date you sought treatment before returning to it.

5. **Inaccurate Or Missing Information** - Railroad injury scenes are chaotic. You may not have reported all your injuries to the captain or supervisor at the time of the injury. As I have stated before, some injury victims are in a state of shock at the initial scene and may not feel the injuries until 24-72 hours afterwards. Some injuries are not as obvious as a fractured skull or artery laceration.

6. **Type of Work You Engage In** - Chances are that if you engage in some type of strenuous or dangerous work that

takes a toil on your body, the insurance company will try to blame your back or neck injuries on your occupation and not the railroad injury. This is another tactic to divert attention away from accepting responsibility for the at-fault driver's negligent behavior.

7.   Completely Denial Of Liability - When an insurance company completely denies your claim then you must hire a personal injury attorney. This situation requires the effective assistance of a lawyer who understands the intricacies of FELA law. Do not simply give up and walk away from the table. Review the section about how to hire a personal injury attorney and follow it. Insurance companies withhold millions of dollars from injured persons each year because the victims are unwilling to follow up. *Below are routine reasons (excuses) employ to deny liability in railroad injuries:*

A. The three year statute of limitations has expired

B. An unknown third-party caused the injury

C. Another known third-party caused the railroad injury

D. An independent witness claims you caused the railroad injury

E. You are 100 percent responsible for causing the railroad injury

F. There is an exclusion for insurance coverage for some reason.

The bottom line in these situations is that no matter what the opposing party says in your case, you need to seek the advice of a lawyer before giving up on compensation for your injuries. If you attempt to handle this matter alone, it is very likely that you will be disappointed by the offer made to you by the at-fault driver's insurance company...and that is if it even offers you a settlement at all.

FELA and Railroad Law Tip:

It is not the railroad's claim agent's goal to maximize your recovery for damages under the FELA. Despite what the claim agent may tell you, the railroad does not pay all your medical bills and the railroad cannot extend the statute of limitations of your FELA claim.

Hiring RJ Alexander Law, PLLC ensures that you will hire a FELA / train wreck attorney who cares about protecting you and your insurance claim. You do not have to fight the insurance company alone! If you have been injured by someone else, call 832-458-1756 or email me at rja@rjalexanderlaw.com for a free no obligation case evaluation.

For additional information on any RJ Alexander Law, PLLC books contact:

RJ Alexander Law, PLLC

7676 Hillmont Street #240Q

Houston, Texas 77040

Phone: (832) 458-1756

Email: rja@rjalexanderlaw.com

RESOURCES

Association of American Railroads: Founded in 1934, AAR is the world's leading railroad policy, research, standard setting, and technology organization that focuses on the safety and productivity of the U.S. freight rail industry. AAR Full members include the major freight railroads in the United States, Canada and Mexico, as well as Amtrak. AAR Railroad Affiliate and Associate Members include non-Class I and commuter railroads, rail supply companies, engineering firms, signal and communications firms, and rail car owners.

Website:https://www.aar.org/

Source: Association of American Railroads

Federal Railroad Administration: The Federal Railroad Administration (FRA) was created by the Department of Transportation Act of 1966. It is one of ten agencies within the U.S. Department of Transportation concerned with intermodal transportation. FRA promotes safe,environmentally sound, successful railroad transportation to meet the needs of all customers today and tomorrow.

Website:https://www.fra.dot.gov/

Source: Federal Railroad Administration

National Labor Relations Board: The National Labor Relations Board is an independent federal agency vested with the power to safeguard employees' rights to organize and to determine whether to have unions as their bargaining representative. The agency also acts to prevent and remedy unfair labor practices committed by private sector employers and unions. **Website:**https://www.nlrb.gov/

Source: National Labor Relations Board

National Transportation Safety Board: The National Transportation Safety Board is an independent Federal agency charged by Congress with investigating every civil aviation accident the United States and significant accidents in other modes of transportation – railroad, highway, marine and pipeline. The NTSB determines the probable cause of the accidents and issues safety recommendations aimed at preventing future accidents. In addition, the NTSB carries out special studies concerning transportation safety and coordinates the resources of the Federal Government and other organizations to provide assistance to victims and their family members impacted by major transportation disasters. **Website:**https://www.ntsb.gov/

Source: National Transportation Safety Board

Pipeline Hazardous Material Safety Administration:

PHMSA's mission is to protect people and the environment by advancing the safe transportation of energy and other hazardous materials that are essential to our daily lives. To do this, the agency establishes national policy, sets and enforces standards, educates, and conducts research to prevent incidents. We also prepare the public and first responders to reduce consequences if an incident does occur.

Website:https://www.phmsa.dot.gov/

Source: Pipeline Hazardous Material Safety Administration

US Department of Homeland Security: Created in the aftermath of the Sept. 11 terrorist attacks, DHS has largely focused on federal preparations to deal with terrorism while trying to manage other duties, including border security, customs and emergency management. The Department of Homeland Security (DHS) was created through the integration of all or part of 22 different federal departments and agencies into a unified, integrated Department, and how DHS has become a more effective and integrated Department, creating a strengthened homeland security enterprise and a more secure

America that is better equipped to confront the range of threats we face. **Website:**https://www.dhs.gov/

Source: U.S. Department of Homeland Security

US Department of Transportation: Department of the U.S. government concerned with transportation and responsible for helping maintain and develop the nation's transportation systems and infrastructure.

Website:https://www.transportation.gov/

Source: U.S. Department of Transportation

US Department of Labor: Responsible for occupational safety, wage and hour standards, unemployment insurance benefits, reemployment services, and some economic statistics. The purpose of the Department of Labor is to foster, promote, and develop the well-being of the wage earners, job seekers, and retirees of the United States; improve working conditions; advance opportunities for profitable employment; and assure work-related benefits and rights.

Website:https://www.dol.gov/

Source: U.S. Department of Labor

Made in the USA
Middletown, DE
21 September 2021